WHERE TO
And Other Scre

WHERE TO LAND

And Other Screenplays

Hal Hartley

ELBORO

ISBN: 978-1-7321817-6-2

Published in New York by Elboro Press

Elboro Press books may be purchased in bulk for educational, business
or sales promotional use. Please address enquiries to:

office@elboropress.com

First Edition, 2021 – First Printing

Where to Land

Where to Land

01. EXTERIOR, CEMETERY

A stately old graveyard in northern Manhattan. Joe Fulton makes his way through the tombstones. He's fifty-eight years old and wears a stylish suit jacket over a casual shirt and jeans. He approaches the groundskeeper, an older man named Leonard loading fallen branches and bundled twigs into a wheelbarrow. Leonard gestures to the tombstones.

> LEONARD
> Can I help you find somebody?

> JOE
> No, thank you. Are you Leonard? I'm
> looking for work.

> LEONARD
> Here in the graveyard?

> JOE
> I live nearby. The superintendent of
> my building is a guy named Oliver.

> LEONARD
> Oliver! Rodriguez? You mean, he ain't
> been arrested yet!

> JOE
> Not yet. He said I should come talk to
> you. You are Leonard, right?

> LEONARD
> *(sets down branches)*
> I am. I am. So, what, you hard up for cash?

> JOE
> No.

> LEONARD
> Sorry, you seem a little too well dressed for
> this line of work.

JOE
(of jacket)
Oh. Yeah. I have an appointment with my
lawyer later this morning.

LEONARD
You mixed up in some bad business?

JOE
She's just helping me draw up my last will
and testament.

LEONARD
So, you're dying.

JOE
No. It's just something you have to do at a
certain point in life, I guess.

LEONARD
(doubtful)
I guess.

JOE
You don't have a will, huh?

LEONARD
Oh, sure. Keep it here.
*(takes a laminated card from
his wallet and reads)*
"If I'm dead call the following number and
please make sure my face is clean and my
mouth and eyes are shut."
(returns it to wallet)
Done. That's my last will and testament. Here,
take this.

He hands Joe his rake and starts away, pushing his wheelbarrow.

JOE
So, is it true: do you need help over here?

LEONARD
Yeah. But the church runs this place and
they can't afford more than one man.

JOE
I don't need to get paid.

LEONARD
(stops, skeptical)
What, is this some kind of charitable
impulse or something?

Joe looks aside and considers this, then—

JOE
No. I don't think so.

LEONARD
Gotta be careful about charitable impulses.
They can be a mask for vanity.

JOE
I suppose.

LEONARD
And complacency.

JOE
No doubt.

LEONARD
(walks on)
So, what do you want to work in the
boneyard for?

JOE
I just need something to do.

LEONARD
(stops again)
Are you a recovering drug addict? An

alcoholic? Is there some kind of substance
abuse issue?

JOE

No, I'm sort of semiretired and I have time
on my hands. I'd like to work outdoors.

LEONARD
(moves on)
You're having yourself a midlife crisis, son.

JOE

Maybe.

LEONARD

What did you do before?

JOE

I directed movies.

LEONARD

Oh yeah? What kind of movies?

JOE

Romantic comedies.

LEONARD
(stops, dubious)
Romantic comedies, huh?

JOE

Yeah, mostly.

LEONARD
(shrugs and moves on)
Now, of course, I ain't the one who does the
hiring. Like I said, the cemetery is owned and
operated by the church up there. A woman by
the name of Alice. She's in the office in the after-
noons. I'll tell her you're coming. What's your
name?

                    JOE

Joe. Joseph Fulton.

                  LEONARD

You ever done this kind of work before?

                    JOE

I have raked leaves. I've mowed lawns.

                  LEONARD

There's more to all this than just raking
leaves and mowing the lawn. This is all
out husbandry.

                    JOE
                 (intrigued)
Husbandry.

                  LEONARD

The care, cultivation and management of
natural resources. You see all these trees,
these hedges, this grass? You let these
things get out of control and the next thing
you know you've got nothing but a small
patch of wilderness, wasteland, an
abandoned garden—the surest sign of a
bankrupt civilization.

                    JOE
                 (impressed)
Understood.

                  LEONARD

The real work around here, day in day out, is
gathering up fallen branches and clearing the
undergrowth that strangles the younger trees.
Then there's the regular mowing and trimming
and raking, of course. But the real hassle are
plastic bags.

They look up at a common plastic shopping bag caught high up in the branches of a tree.

                              JOE
                How do you deal with that?

Leonard takes a slingshot out of his back pocket, finds a rock,
aims, and fires. The plastic bag is torn cleanly out of the branches.
Joe is entertained. But Leonard waits and listens. The bag plum-
mets to earth fifty yards away. He nods, satisfied, and moves on.

                            LEONARD
                There's often collateral damage—someone's
                windshield or whatnot. And you gotta find the
                right kind of stone, one with wide flat surfaces
                so it don't just tear a hole in the offending
                plastic bag, but catches it, gains some purchase
                on it, and brings it down.
                        (continues on)
                And look, the thing to keep in mind is what
                every farmer knows: no matter how many
                times you cut the grass it's gonna need to be
                cut again. Same with the leaves and these
                fucking plastic bags.

02. INTERIOR, SUBWAY

Joe rides the subway downtown.

03. EXTERIOR, MIDTOWN MANHATTAN

Joe makes his way through the traffic and crowded sidewalks.

04. INTERIOR, LAW OFFICE

Joe listens as his lawyer, a sharp-witted woman not much younger
than himself, explains—

                            LAURA
                Simply stated, a last will and testament is
                a legal document that lets you designate
                individuals or charities to receive your

property and possessions when you pass
away. These individuals and charities are
referred to as beneficiaries.

                    JOE
                (nods)
Okay. So far so good.

                   LAURA
A last will also allows you, for instance, to
name a guardian to care for your underage
children.

                    JOE
I have no children.

Laura looks up over the top of her reading glasses.

                   LAURA
That you know of.

                    JOE
                (piqued)
What are you trying to say?

                   LAURA
Only that one needs to be careful. You
weren't always the quiet and unassuming
elder statesman of American romantic
comedy, kiddo. I recall a lot of broken
hearts. Just gotta make sure there are no
skeletons in the closets. No disgruntled
scion loitering in the halls of justice.

                    JOE
Wow. Why even make stories up at all?
Life itself is so rife with contention!

                   LAURA
Tell me about it. There'd be nothing for
us lawyers to do otherwise. Listen, the main

purpose of a will is to ensure that your wishes, and not the default laws of the state, will be followed upon your death.

JOE

How do we begin?

LAURA

The paperwork is pretty standard. I can get started on that. You, meanwhile, need to go home and make a list of your possessions, property, and the individuals or charities you would like to leave them to when you die. You still married?

JOE

No.

LAURA

(taking notes)
Formally divorced?

JOE

I paid the state what they said they were owed and I have a receipt to prove it.

LAURA

(sets down pen)
How is she?

JOE

Clara?

LAURA

Your wife.

JOE

My ex-wife.

LAURA

I so liked her. How could you blow that?

                           JOE
We were young. We were in love. We
changed.

                          LAURA
You still dating the superhero?

                           JOE
Muriel. Yes.

                          LAURA
And what are her expectations?

                           JOE
Her expectations of what?

                          LAURA
Look, I know Muriel Hoffman is a famous
and wealthy television star. But it's not all
about money, you know. Most importantly,
of course, are the rights in your movies.
Intellectual property. Those rights can be
left to your designated beneficiaries: Clara?
Muriel? Both? Neither? All or just some?
None at all? The potential for heartbreak
and scandal is, of course, endless.

                           JOE
Wow, is this what it all comes down to?

                          LAURA
I'm afraid so. Somewhere along the
line you generated a list of material and
intellectual assets people might want to
fight about later. Here's a list of things you
need to address. Go home and think about it.

05. INTERIOR, SUBWAY

Joe rides the train home, thinking about it, studying the brochure
Laura gave him.

06. EXTERIOR, NEIGHBORHOOD

Joe comes up to the street from the subway heads towards a cafe.

07. INTERIOR, CAFE

Joe enters. The waitress, Anna, greets him in passing—

> ANNA
>
> Hi Joe.

> JOE
>
> Hey, Anna. A double espresso. Thanks.

Joe takes a seat at a table and can't help overhearing two busy young men at a nearby table, an aspiring television writer pitching an idea to his producer friend.

> MICK
>
> Season two, episode one: they're back
> together again.

> KEITH
>
> Really?

> MICK
>
> Just an idea.

> KEITH
>
> I think the network wants something more
> bleak.

> MICK
>
> Less comforting?

> KEITH
>
> Yeah. Darker.

> MICK
>
> But it's a... I mean, it's still a half hour
> comedy, right?

KEITH

Yeah. Sure. Just they're not into likeable
characters. We gotta skew towards
recognizably selfish and unreliable types.
It's more realistic.

MICK

More natural?

KEITH

Don't mix things up.

MICK

Right.

Muriel enters dramatically. She's a beautiful woman and clearly a
movie star. She stops, lowers her sunglasses and approaches Joe.
He stands to greet her and she buries herself in his chest. Everyone in the cafe looks on, touched and starstruck. Meanwhile—

KEITH

Have you ever heard of the second law
of thermodynamics?

MICK

Vaguely.

KEITH

All energy is in the process of burning itself
out. Heat is created by the dying of energy.
You can create a third energy by the
destruction of two other energies. It's the
same with relationships. Two people come
together to form this passion, love, trust,
polyamorous transgender confusion—
whatever. But in so doing they destroy one
another. And this mutual destruction yields
a new energy.

MICK

The story!

KEITH

More specifically: season two.

MICK
(makes note)
Yeah, that's how it is: people destroy one another!

KEITH

It's really just physics.

MICK

Got it.

KEITH
(spots Muriel)
Oh, wow.

MICK

What?

KEITH

Is that? It is. That's...

MICK
(whispers reverently)
Muriel Hoffman!

KEITH

The Invincible Allura!

At Joe's table, Muriel sobs quietly. He tries to console her.

JOE

I'm fine. Don't be so dramatic. This is just something a responsible adult is supposed to do: make a will. My lawyers have been telling me to do it for twenty-five years.

MURIEL

But why now?

                    JOE
        If not now, when? I have the time.

Joe notices Keith and Mick watching. Caught, they turn away.
Muriel blows her nose.

                  MURIEL
        You know something don't you?

                    JOE
        No. I mean, yes: I'm a perfectly healthy
        fifty-eight-year-old guy.

                  MURIEL
        Frank Zappa died at fifty-eight.

                    JOE
        Really?

                  MURIEL
        Brecht.

                    JOE
        Don't remind me.

                  MURIEL
        Dickens.

                    JOE
        London was an unhealthy smog-laden place
        in the eighteen-sixties.

                  MURIEL
        Molière.

                    JOE
        That was the 17th century! He was an old
        man by then.

                  MURIEL
        And what about me?

JOE
(careful)
Well, I don't want to assume anything, but:
are you okay?

MURIEL
(quietly hysterical)
Am I okay? How can you ask me that! No, I'm
not okay. The man I love is busy making his
last will and testament and... and...

ANNA
(interrupts)
Anything for you, Miss Hoffman?

MURIEL
(bravely)
Yes. Thank you. Tea. Earl Grey.

Joe reaches across the table and takes her hand.

JOE
What's really troubling you?

MURIEL
(hesitates)
Is there a future for us?

JOE
I hope so.

MURIEL
(sighs, looks away)
I need an anchor.

08. EXTERIOR, CAFE

Keith and Mick exit, Keith scrolling through his smartphone.

KEITH
If that's Muriel Hoffman, that guy's gotta be...

MICK
Oh, yeah, what's his name.

KEITH
I've heard of him.

MICK
He made that film...

KEITH
The one about the guy...

MICK
And the girl he loves...

KEITH
Who works in a factory.

MICK
And the hand grenade.

KEITH
Really?

MICK
I think so. Maybe not.

KEITH
Whatever.
          (finds what he's looking for)
Yeah, look!

He displays the phone and Mick reads—.

MICK
Joe Fulton?

KEITH
He's won awards and shit, apparently.

Mick looks back inside, troubled.

MICK

That's Joseph Fulton, huh?

KEITH

Lucky bastard. He's too old for her. There's
no justice in this world, Mick.

MICK

Come on. We need to talk.

Mick walks off and Keith follows, intrigued.

09. INTERIOR, CAFE

Muriel stands and puts her coat back on, preparing to leave.

MURIEL

I have a photo shoot. There's a car waiting.
Will I see you later?

JOE

Come to the apartment.

MURIEL

Okay. Are you staying?

JOE

I have an interview in ten minutes. Someone
writing a book.

MURIEL

Don't exhaust yourself.

JOE

Muriel, I'm fine.

MURIEL

You're pale.

JOE

Am I?

MURIEL

Preoccupied. Distant...

JOE

Enough. Please. I love you.

MURIEL

You're too brave.

She kisses him, turns and exits with a flourish. Joe looks around at the cafe's other patrons who are all thoroughly entertained and moved.

10. INTERIOR, BAR

Keith and Mick have migrated to their local bar across the street. Mick is troubled, moved, and confused. Keith is just amazed.

KEITH

Are you fucking kidding me!

MICK

(explains)

My mom raised me on her own. I never
knew who my father was. She never told
me. But whenever she had a little too much
to drink she'd get sentimental and go on
about having had this big affair with this
film director named Joe Fulton.

Keith finds a pair of binoculars behind the bar and moves to the front window.

KEITH

In New York?

MICK

Yeah. She was an actress back in the day.

KEITH

It's gotta be him, man.

MICK

(worried)

Fuck.

KEITH

What are you so down about? Go talk to the
guy. He might be loaded. You might be in line
for an inheritance.

MICK

(reconsiders)

You think he's worth anything?

KEITH

Got a pretty long resume. He's dating Muriel
Hoffman.

MICK

(lightens up)

You see the last episode of Allura?

KEITH

Fucking genius!

MICK

When the guy with the thing...

KEITH

Tries to kill her by putting that thing in the
other thing...

MICK

And then she, at the last minute...

KEITH

In that outfit from season three!

MICK

Wow!

They toast to her and drink.

KEITH

She's awesome.

MICK

I wrote that miniseries for her.

KEITH

About the nun?

MICK

With psychic powers.

KEITH

And the convent?

MICK

Where they make beer.

KEITH

And shelter illegal immigrants from trans-
national capitalist aggression?

MICK

I can change that to something less
controversial.

KEITH

No. No. Controversy can be useful. But
anyway... Wow, she'd be perfect!

MICK

Right?

KEITH

Well, now she's like your aunt.

MICK

Keith, don't mess with me!

KEITH

I mean it. You got total direct access to

Muriel Hoffman because she's like your
dad's main squeeze.

                    MICK
You really think he's my dad?

                    KEITH
It's worth asking.

Keith orders another round from the bartender, Ignatius.

11. INTERIOR, CAFE

A young academic named Emily is with Joe.

                    EMILY
I'm writing a book about your films and want
to give you the opportunity to engage with me
in a series of one-on-one interviews that will,
you know, amplify the issues I treat and the
points I make in the main text.

                    JOE
                (patiently)
I don't think so. But thanks. Thanks for being
interested enough to write about my films.

                    EMILY
It would really make the book special.

                    JOE
But it's your book. You can make a book
about my films. You don't need my
permission. However, I wouldn't want my
contribution to it to seem like an endorsement
of your ideas. Your ideas about my films are
your ideas about my films. Good luck.

She's disappointed and pouts. A leather-clad rocker Joe's age,
Eric, enters and gives Joe a fist bump before moving on to the
counter.

EMILY
(persists)
But there are a number of other books about
your films and, if I'm going to interest a
publisher, I need to make this one different.

JOE
Ah. Yes, I understand.

EMILY
But have no sympathy.

JOE
Well, hey, look, it's tough all over. Like I
said, I appreciate your interest in my work.
And I thank you for being frank about your
situation. But I can't help you out there.

She sits back, folds her arms, and assesses Joe professionally.

EMILY
Yes, you make great use of frankness as a
technique of ironic comment—in the films.

JOE
Do I?

EMILY
I explain all this in a footnote to chapter four,
section three: It's ironical. Satirical. Your films
demonstrate a sinister dexterity in relation to
the audience. The comic attitudes deal in
double meanings and insinuation—
(stops herself)
It's a long footnote.

Impressed, Joe looks to Eric to see if he's heard this. He has. He
nods and turns away. Joe decides to hear more.

JOE
Anna, a glass of red wine, please. Thank you.

12. INTERIOR, BAR

Leonard enters and sits at the bar. He shakes hands with Ignatius. Keith is still spying on Joe across the street in the cafe while Mick finishes on his mobile device with his mom.

> MICK
> *(exhausted)*
> Okay. Okay, Mom. No problem. I'll see you in a few weeks. Yeah. Bye.

> KEITH
> What she say? Is Joe Fulton your dad?

> MICK
> She don't remember.

> KEITH
> She don't *remember*?

> MICK
> Yeah, she dated Joe Fulton a number of times. But there was this actor too from a commercial she did and then this teenager who worked on the boat belonging to this big record company executive.
> *(takes binoculars)*
> But she's pretty sure it's not the record company executive.

> KEITH
> So that leaves the teenager, the actor or Fulton.

Leonard looks over.

> LEONARD
> Fulton? Joe Fulton?

> MICK
> Yeah, why? You know him?

LEONARD
He applied for a job over there today.

Mick and Keith look to Ignatius.

IGNATIUS
(explains)
Leonard works in the graveyard.

MICK
The graveyard! No, can't be the same guy.

LEONARD
Nicely dressed, late fifties, educated
somewhat. But it's been a while since he's
handled a rake, if you know what I mean.

KEITH
Why would he be applying for a job in a
cemetery?

LEONARD
Well, he ain't doing it for the money.

KEITH
That's suspicious.

LEONARD
And it ain't a charitable type thing.

KEITH
What, so like he's doing it for his health?

LEONARD
Maybe.

KEITH
Mighty suspicious.

LEONARD
I think it's a spiritual thing.

Inspired, Keith looks from Mick to Ignatius and then returns to Leonard.

                    KEITH
          You mean—you mean like a man—like a
          man at the end of his life?

                    MICK
          Keith, shut up!

                    KEITH
          Mick, trust me. I've seen stuff like this on
          YouTube. People approach the end of their
          lives and they start feeling the need to get
          close to nature!

                    IGNATIUS
          Yeah, I saw that one. Sixteen thousand
          views.

                    KEITH
          He's dying! I'm sure of it! We gotta make a
          move. He still over there?

Mick turns away from the window, despondent.

                    MICK
          He's with that professor woman still.

                    KEITH
          Maybe you just gotta go ask him yourself.

                    MICK
          What, like, if he's dying?

                    KEITH
          No! If you're his son.

                    MICK
                  (sits at bar)
          I don't look nothing like him anyway.

13. INTERIOR, CAFE

Joe listens as Emily finishes her impromptu lecture. Everyone in the cafe is paying studious attention.

> EMILY
>
> Ultimately, its comedy lies in the showing
> of what is perfectly obvious to any thinking
> person. Thoughtful people laugh because it's
> a shock to be reminded how the obvious is
> avoided in everyday life. Unthoughtful people
> are maybe a little unsettled, not sure if they
> understand. Perhaps they're even threatened.
> But being uncertain, even threatened, is the
> beginning of thinking.

Anna nods and makes a note of this in her receipt pad.

> EMILY
> *(continues)*
> Rather, the films are, if I may say so, sincere
> propaganda against ignorance rather than
> ironic commentary about devious intelligence.

Joe sits back, genuinely impressed, and looks to Eric who nods thoughtfully, equally impressed.

> JOE
>
> Interesting.

The cafe patrons applaud.

> EMILY
>
> Finally, Mister Fulton...
> *(acknowledges patrons)*
> Thank you. Thank you.
> *(back to Joe)*
> Finally, I think I agree with you. You yourself
> have no strong or compelling notions about
> your own work. And I mean that, in terms of
> hermeneutics, in a positive way.

Joe's not sure what she means, but accepts it as a complement.

                    JOE
          Thank you.

                    EMILY
          You're welcome.

                    JOE
          So, you don't need to interview me?

                    EMILY
          I'm afraid not. No. Sorry.

Joe is relieved. He stands and pays for their drinks.

                    JOE
          No harm done. I gotta go. Good luck with
          your book.

He high-fives Eric as he passes by the counter and leaves.

14. INTERIOR, BODEGA

Joe enters and nods to the proprietor, Octavio, who is watching
the television above the counter.

                    JOE
          Hola Octavio.

Octavio shakes his head, despondent.

                    OCTAVIO
                 (of news)
          Joe, where will it end! Tell me, please.
                 (to a teenager)
          Hey, my friend, you gonna buy that or what?

                    JOE
          Octavio, you've got to stop watching the
          news. It's not good for you.

Off to the side, selling the lottery tickets, is Octavio's curvaceous cousin, Alejandra.

ALEJANDRA
Tell him, Joe! He's addicted!

OCTAVIO
(defends himself)
A person needs to know what's going on in the world!

ALEJANDRA
Why? What difference will it make if you know all these things? What are you going to do about it? You think these terrorists, politicians and businessmen will come and ask: 'Octavio, what is your opinion about all this stuff?'

Joe stops at the beer cooler and pauses.

JOE
(discovers a new beer)
What's this?

OCTAVIO
Extra Ultra Lights. New. Only 62 calories per bottle.

JOE
Any good?

OCTAVIO
My wife, she says nothing else no more for me. The end of the world. Nine dollars.

JOE
Affordable too! I'll try it out.

ALEJANDRA
Are you watching your figure too, Joe?

                              JOE
Somebody has to, Alejandra.

                           ALEJANDRA
Yeah, well, you have a pretty girlfriend so
you should work hard to deserve her. You
find no sympathy here, señor.

                              JOE
None?

                           ALEJANDRA
                    (relents)
Okay. Maybe a little. Next!

15. INTERIOR, JOE'S APARTMENT

Joe enters with the groceries, sorting through his mail. He drops
the mail on the kitchen counter, twists the cap off a beer, and
surveys his small but well-appointed kitchen. He steps back out
into the hall and leans in the doorway of his studio. It's a combi-
nation office and workshop with a writing desk, a computer, a
piano and a few electric guitars. He then heads down the short
hall, dominated by an old schoolroom blackboard hung on the
wall like a piece of art, and moves to the far end of the apartment.
Stopping in the doorway there, he considers his bedroom. The
walls are lined floor to ceiling with books. It is, in fact, a library
with a bed. Turning back away, he opens the door to the bathroom. It too is populated with books. Finally, he returns to the
kitchen and sits at the little table. He takes a notebook from his
inside jacket pocket and sets to work with a pencil.

                              JOE
Okay.
                    (writing)
One small table. Marble, brass.

He sits back and considers the table then stands and crosses to the
counter. He finds a retractable tape measure in the drawer, comes
back, and measures the small cafe table. Satisfied, he sits and continues writing—

                              30

                           JOE
        Twenty inches in diameter. Two chairs,
        matching, wood.

This accomplished, he looks up from his notebook. His gaze falls
upon the clock on the wall. There's a knock at the door.

16. INTERIOR, JOE'S APARTMENT

Opening the door, Joe discovers the building's superintendent.

                           JOE
        Hey, Oliver.

                         OLIVER
        Joe, you got hot water?

                           JOE
        I did this morning.

Oliver comes right in, goes to the kitchen sink, and runs the tap.

                         OLIVER
        No. Nothing.
                    (shuts off tap)
        Those slobs at the management company
        gotta face facts and get a new boiler, man.
        This can't keep happening. What with the
        cold weather coming on.
                    (spots Joe's beer)
        What's this?

                           JOE
        Extra Ultra Light.

                         OLIVER
                    (reads label)
        Only 62 calories per bottle.

                           JOE
        It's the new thing.

OLIVER

Beer flavored water.

JOE
(hands him one)

Here.

OLIVER

Thanks. Listen, can you sign my petition?
I'm running for city council.

JOE

For real this time?

OLIVER

For this district, yeah.

JOE

As an anarchist?

OLIVER

At least strongly socialist. I'll see what I can
get away with. We gotta stop this gentrification
crap or my mom and her sisters will be out on
the street by Christmas next year.
(of beer)
This ain't half bad.

They clink bottles as Joe passes over to the window, sighing.

JOE

Property.

OLIVER

It's all about property, man.

JOE

"Ownership is bondage."

OLIVER

Who said that first?

JOE

Proudhon, I think. French. Mid-nineteenth
century.

OLIVER

Anarchist?

JOE

The original, I guess.

OLIVER

How do you spell that?

Joe writes it in his notebook and tears out the page.

OLIVER
(reads)
"Proudhon."

JOE

There's some of his stuff in English on the
shelves in the bathroom.

Oliver goes straight off to the bathroom.

OLIVER

Where's he at?

JOE

On the right somewhere. Opposite the sink.

Joe opens the kitchen cabinets, counts his dishes, and writes in the
book—

JOE

Six dinner plates. Four smaller plates. Two
soup bowls.

OLIVER
(returns with book)
Got it!

Joe is staring into his kitchen drawer.

JOE
Where did all this silverware come from?

OLIVER
(impressed)
Wow, this shit's real.

JOE
How do we acquire so much stuff?

OLIVER
What stuff! Dude, you got nothing in this
place but books and the tools you use to
make a living with.

JOE
But I do own the place.

OLIVER
Sure, but you live here. It's not like these
rinky-dink would-be real estate tycoons who
buy the apartments just to let them out on
short term leases until they can charge enough
to be free of the rent control laws.

JOE
You know, I spent every day of my life since
the age of thirty trying not to be possessive.

OLIVER
Why?

JOE
The love of a girl, mostly. Her beauty,
companionship, etcetera. I made myself sick
for a year and a half because I couldn't possess
her—to own her undying devotion, so I could
announce to the world that this here lovely
woman was mine.

OLIVER

Your emotional life was corrupted by the
profit motive.

JOE

Could be.

OLIVER

How'd you get over it?

JOE

I met another beautiful girl whose expectations
I took advantage of myself. I hurt her feelings
badly and realized I'd done to her what this
other girl had done to me.

Oliver places the petition on the table with a pen.

OLIVER

Laissez faire capitalism of the soul. Every man
for himself! Dude, you're lucky you survived.
(of petition)
Here. Sign there.

JOE

(signing petition)
I live with it still, that sin. She bought me that
clock for some reason, on a trip to Amsterdam.

OLIVER

Having a conscience is one thing, Joe, but
don't get all masochistic about it.

JOE

(hands back petition)
It's a good clock.

OLIVER

Put your shoulder to the wheel! Labor with
gratitude! That is the whole of the law,
comrade! See you later.

He leaves. Joe sips his beer and looks at his list.

17. INTERIOR, JOE'S APARTMENT

A little later, the front door is opened a crack and a twenty-year-old girl named Veronica peeks in, jiggling her set of keys.

> VERONICA
Hola! I'm here!

> JOE
Sobrina!

> VERONICA
Are you decent? *Tio? Mon Oncle?*

> JOE
Wie geht es ihnen!

> VERONICA
> *(finds him)*
Ah! There you are.

> JOE
You're early.

> VERONICA
Afternoon class was canceled. So, what is this Oliver is saying: you're retiring?

> JOE
> *(amused)*
Ha! If I were only allowed!

> VERONICA
> *(like an angry parent)*
You are not allowed! I insist!
> *(sitting)*
Listen to this, I found it today:
> *(reads from tablet)*
"To be happy: learn how to do something."

                              JOE

    See, I told you so.

                           VERONICA

    You did?

He stands and places his empty beer bottle beneath the sink.

                              JOE

    One way or another, always.

                           VERONICA

    What's the last thing you learned how
    to do?

                              JOE

    How to remove plastic bags from high
    up in the branches of a tree.

                           VERONICA
                          (surprised)
    Oh. I was expecting it to have something
    to do with an app on your phone.

                              JOE

    I'm still trying to learn how to turn that
    thing on and off. Come: what's the subject
    of your essay?

                           VERONICA
                       (searches tablet, then)
    "Do we learn more from our mistakes or
     from our successful actions?"

                              JOE

    What do you think?

                           VERONICA
                         (thinks, then)
    Successful action. We learn more from
    success than failure.

                               37

JOE

That may be true. But it's also not the
question. Failure is not mentioned. Though,
mistakes are.

VERONICA

Are mistakes not failures?

JOE
(intrigued)
Okay, now that's interesting!
(checks the time)
But I've got an appointment at the church.
Work on it. We'll continue on Friday. Lock
up when you leave.

VERONICA

The church! Are you getting married or
something?

JOE

No. It's about the cemetery.

He kisses her on the head and leaves. As Veronica sets about be-
ginning her essay, the phone rings. She runs and answers it, pretending to be a receptionist.

VERONICA
(into phone)
The offices of Mister Joseph Fulton. How may
I direct your call?

18. INTERIOR, SOUNDSTAGE

(Intercut with previous scene) Dressed in her Invincible Allura
costume—sort of a Steam Punk Wonder Woman type thing—
Muriel is having her hair and makeup attended to.

MURIEL
(dramatically suspicious)
Who is this?

VERONICA

Who may I say is calling?

MURIEL

Muriel.

VERONICA

Oh! Muriel! It's Veronica, Joe's niece.

MURIEL

Oh. Hello, Veronica. I'm sorry. For a moment
I thought maybe Joe had another woman in
his life and that he was taking terrible
advantage of my affections.

VERONICA

Oh, not at all. Just me.

MURIEL

Is he there?

VERONICA

No, he's gone to a meeting at the church.

MURIEL

The church?

VERONICA

Yes, something about the cemetery.

Muriel falls into her makeup chair.

MURIEL

I knew it!

VERONICA

Knew what?

MURIEL

He hasn't said anything to you—to your
family?

VERONICA

About what?

MURIEL

His health.

Now Veronica is worried.

VERONICA

No. Why? Is there something we should know?

MURIEL

Veronica, are you seated?

VERONICA

No. Wait. Hold on.
(she sits)
Okay. I'm seated.

MURIEL

Your uncle is having his last will and testament
drawn up.

VERONICA

Oh?

MURIEL

It's true. Though he pretends it's just a
formality.

VERONICA

And now he's gone to the church.

MURIEL

To discuss the cemetery.

VERONICA

Which means—

MURIEL

A burial plot—

VERONICA

His final resting place!

Muriel is directed to return to set.

MURIEL

Veronica, I have to go. We must talk more.
Come to me.

Veronica hangs up. Her eyes fall on the mail Joe left on the counter. Sorting through it, she finds a letter from the Mount Saint Pleasant Hospital and Research Clinic. It's stamped *confidential*. Torn, she hesitates, but then takes the envelope and her backpack and leaves.

19. INTERIOR, CHURCH OFFICES

Joe sits across from a thoughtful woman in her forties, Alice, one of the church's part-time volunteers.

ALICE

So why do you want this kind of work?

JOE

I want to do something useful and perennial.

ALICE

Perennial?

JOE

Yes. Something, some service or labor, that
is constantly and forever required. Continually
recurring.

ALICE

Yes, I know what perennial means. Thank
you. You don't think you're overqualified
for the position?

JOE

Of assistant groundskeeper?

ALICE

Yes.

JOE

No, in fact, I think my thirty-year career as a
writer, director and producer of motion pictures
qualifies me perfectly to be an assistant
groundskeeper.

ALICE

Well, I'm in no position to know. But...
(lifts his application)
Are you religiously observant Mister Fulton?

JOE

No. But I've been described as spiritually
curious.

ALICE

By whom?

JOE

Le Monde.

ALICE

Le Monde?

JOE

French newspaper.

ALICE

Ah, I see.

JOE

Are you?

ALICE

Am I what?

JOE

Religiously observant.

ALICE
(thinks about it)
I'm observant. I wonder more and more if I'm
religious. I'm comforted by the routine, by the
ceremony, by the arcane gestures. The very
uselessness of them. It stops time somehow,
lets me breathe. But I tend to lose interest when
I listen to the liturgy. The spell gets broken.
So, I attend high mass in Latin on Sunday
morning. I don't know Latin and so it all
remains—as my husband says—mumbo
jumbo. But it remains beautiful because of its
unintelligibility and practical uselessness.
Still, I feel peace within me and around me
at those times.

Joe watches her think her own thoughts. Finally—

ALICE
Well, Mister Fulton. I'll submit your
application at our church council meeting
later today and let you know our decision.

JOE
Thank you.

20. INTERIOR, CHURCH

Exiting the offices, Joe finds himself in the chapel itself. He
makes his way along the central nave and passes his neighbor, an
older man named Tom Webster, who is startled to see Joe in the
church.

21. EXTERIOR, STREET

Minutes later, Veronica is waiting to cross the street, studying the
envelope from the hospital.

TOM
(approaches)
Miss Fulton!

VERONICA
(startled, looks up)
Oh, hi Mister Webster.

TOM
Is everything all right? You look concerned.

VERONICA
(hesitates)
It's about my uncle.

Tom ushers her aside and out of the middle of the sidewalk.

TOM
I was very surprised to see him in church just
now.

VERONICA
Yes. He had a meeting there to discuss—the,
the cemetery.

Tom seems to understand the whole tragic picture now. He takes
her hand and consoles her.

TOM
The cemetery.

VERONICA
And there's a letter.
(reveals the envelope)
From the hospital.

Tom stands back, looks around, and sighs.

TOM
Good god! He's such a stoic!

22. INTERIOR, SOUNDSTAGE

Muriel, in her Invincible Allura costume, is being interviewed by
a young male journalist.

INTERVIEWER
Miss Hoffman, can we expect a 14th season
of *The Invincible Allura*?

MURIEL
I don't know.

INTERVIEWER
(stunned)
But it is hugely popular. One of the most
successful television series in history.

MURIEL
Yes. And I'm grateful. But I might want to
do other things?

INTERVIEWER
Why?

MURIEL
Being a female superhero with an adoring
worldwide fan base can take up a lot of
space.

INTERVIEWER
Space?

MURIEL
In my life.

INTERVIEWER
You've famously said your work was your
life.

MURIEL
Yes. Yes, I know. But... Maybe there's a time
when one's life must become one's work.
I don't know.

INTERVIEWER
What other things would you do?

MURIEL

It's been a long time since I played someone
without the power of a hundred men, without
the sex appeal of a fashion model and the
mental capacity of a really high-end
smartphone. It would be interesting to play a
regular human being—with problems, of
course. You know, like a mom. A single
mom. A single mom with a drinking problem.
A single mom with a drinking problem and
a certain talent for, say, solving crime. You
know, something normal like that.
        (then, having more ideas)
Or...

INTERVIEWER

Excuse me?

MURIEL

Maybe...

INTERVIEWER

Yes?

MURIEL

I could be a woman. A woman who loves a
man. A man whose life she shares and whose
life he too shares in return. A couple, so to
speak, moving through life together, side by
side. Arguing, of course, struggling. But with
the knowledge that they're inseparable, bound
to one another by things larger and more
intimate than their differences.

INTERVIEWER

Marriage?

MURIEL

Perhaps. But more fluid. More dynamic.
There would be tragedy, of course. Missed
opportunities. Moral complexities too

unexpected to reconcile without a collapse
into profound solitude and introspection.
But funny too.

Her producer interrupts—

PRODUCER
Muriel, the photographer is here. And your
guest.

MURIEL
Veronica!

They rush into one another's arms.

23. EXTERIOR, NEIGHBORHOOD

Joe hurries along to another meeting and notices Mick and Keith
following him. Seeing they've been spotted they duck into an
alley and hide. Joe moves on.

24. INTERIOR, ELIZABETH'S APARTMENT

A home care helper named Inez greets Joe at the door. She shows
him into a room where a slow-moving but alert elderly woman
sits by the window reading the newspaper with a magnifying
glass. She looks up as he enters.

ELIZABETH
Who is it?

JOE
Elizabeth. You look great!

ELIZABETH
(hard of hearing)
What?

JOE
I said you look very, very good for a person
who is one hundred years old.

She allows herself to be embraced. Afterwards, Joe stands back. She studies him.

> ELIZABETH
> You were expecting to find me on my death bed, admit it. And don't flirt with me, Joe Fulton. I know how you are with the ladies.

> JOE
> I brought you a cigar.

> ELIZABETH
> Oh! You're a good one, Joe.
> *(sniffs the cigar)*
> I'm not allowed to smoke them anymore, you know.

> JOE
> I figured as much.

> ELIZABETH
> But I like to have them around. Sit down. Sit down.

Joe sits on the couch across from her.

> JOE
> Listen, I might need a character reference.

> ELIZABETH
> You? Who's questioning your character?

> JOE
> The church up near me. I want to work in their graveyard as a groundskeeper.

> ELIZABETH
> Interesting.

> JOE
> I think so.

ELIZABETH
(of newspaper)
Listen, tell me about this United Nations report
on climate change that came out yesterday.
What do you know?

JOE
It's bad. We've got about twenty years before
we're fighting street to street for clean water.
Inland will become desert. Mass migration.
The breakdown of civil institutions. The works.

She mulls this over and lights the cigar without thinking, out of
habit.

ELIZABETH
Boy, I wish I could be around to see that. But
I probably won't be.

JOE
It won't be pretty. I was kind of hoping I'd be
dead and gone myself before it got that bad.
But now it looks like I'll be an eighty-year-old
tagging along behind the young folk hoping to
be useful somehow.
(studies the bookshelves)
Why do you want to hang around to see
society descend into barbarism?

ELIZABETH
(thinks, smokes, then)
Change is always interesting. Of course,
there will be reaction to barbarism too, you
see. What will that be like this time around?
I made some of my best friends as a
teenager fighting the fascists in Europe.
Twenty-five years later I was arrested with
a crowd of students here at Columbia
University—still fighting fascists in a way.
But differently. The brutality was less overt
—unless of course you happened to be a

black person...

(loses her train of thought)

What was I saying?

JOE

Change.

ELIZABETH

Yes, and it's always technological.

JOE

How so?

ELIZABETH

It's our technology that evolves, not our moral or ethical selves. All things considered, there's not much difference between the ancient Babylonians and ourselves. Our ethics adapt to our technology. It's like the Swiss philosopher said...

JOE

Rousseau?

ELIZABETH

No, the other one. Twentieth century...
No matter. "Who needs a plastic cup? Who needs an atomic bomb?"

(smokes, then)

Say what you will, but how you answer these questions tells you a lot about yourself and your expectations of others.

(pauses, turns to Joe)

Joe, forgive me, I should know this: do you have children?

JOE

No. I have nieces and nephews.

ELIZABETH

Are you saddened by what you suspect they'll

have to go through?

JOE

Yes.

ELIZABETH

Is that why you want to be an assistant groundskeeper in a graveyard?

JOE

Somehow.

He finds a particular book on the shelves and brings it down.

JOE
(reads title)
"Self-Emptying and World Maintenance".

ELIZABETH

Someone gave that to me years ago, a rabbi.

JOE
(re-shelves book)
That's got something to do with it maybe:
world maintenance, yes. But being merely
useful—sustainable—is not enough. It
misses the point somehow. I don't want to
merely exist, I want to—yes—change.
(sits, opens notebook)
I met a fascinating person earlier. Alice.
She works at the church. She used a lovely
phrase: "practical uselessness."

ELIZABETH

That's the self-emptying part.

JOE

How do you mean?

She stands up out of her chair slowly and moves carefully to the
window.

ELIZABETH

We've got to be practical, of course. We must
do what we have to do to live.
(pauses, concerned)
Where's my cigar?

JOE

In your hand.

ELIZABETH

Oh.
(smokes, then)
But the notion that all we do should amount
to something else, something more valuable,
something transferable, something profitably
disposable—that, in fact, it should accumulate
capital: this is the opposite of self-emptying.
This is to conceive of oneself and one's work
as tradeable material goods.
(moves to window)
But a lot of us suspect we are more than just
material—that we are, in fact, ephemeral,
passing, fundamentally immaterial. And it's
in that practical uselessness, engaging with
reality without the imperative to gain thereby—
that's where we do, really, engage in life and,
yes, burn like the flame of a candle and so on.
Okay.
(returns to chair)
The rest, as someone once said, is just
plumbing!

JOE

Now how do I say that to my twenty-year-
old niece and be understood?

ELIZABETH

Do you still worry about being understood?

JOE

Maybe not. Sometimes.

ELIZABETH

You grow out of it. Enjoy their ingenuity, the
young. Encourage them. But stay out of their
way.
(glances at newspaper)
Bad times are coming, yes. But good things
do get done.
(nods, remembering)
We are on the outside, those of us without
children. It was a choice, I'm sure, somehow,
to resist too much involvement, too much
dedication to individuals, so we could see
more clearly, perhaps. So we could remain
uncompromised.
(shakes her head clear)
I worked in a dry cleaner's for twenty years
while I wrote my first book. Starched shirts
and pressed slacks might seem a long way
from self-emptying and world maintenance,
but it helped.
(smokes, then)
You still dating the superhero?

Before Joe can answer, Elizabeth looks up at the entranceway.
Inez stands there, hands on hips, frowning. Caught, Elizabeth lays
down her cigar.

25. INTERIOR, SOUNDSTAGE

Veronica sits aside while Muriel models her costume. The photographer and his assistants buzz around her, making adjustments,
giving directions and touch-ups. Muriel studies the envelope from
the hospital. She resists her impulse to open it and hands it back to
Veronica.

MURIEL
(strikes a pose)
When did you see him last?

VERONICA
Today. An hour ago.

The lights flash, the camera clicks, and Muriel vogues absently.

MURIEL
And you didn't think he looked—wistful?

VERONICA
Wistful?

MURIEL
Melancholy?

Veronica shrugs and sits back down.

VERONICA
Well, melancholia's his thing. He's made a
good career out of it. He says so all the time.

PHOTOGRAPHER
Muriel, please, this way. Thanks.

Muriel poses. Flashes ensue. She moves on.

MURIEL
Of course. But he's a bit more pensive recently,
like a man—like a man paralyzed by the
fleetingness of life, struck dumb by an
awareness of his final absence, his inevitable
passing.

VERONICA
He does talk a lot more about the terrible
beauty of nature's disregard for the human.

MURIEL
(stops, turns, points)
Exactly!

PHOTOGRAPHER
Perfect! Hold that!

And she holds that pose as she effusively elaborates—

MURIEL

This heartbreaking preoccupation with the
meaninglessness of human endeavor!

VERONICA

He wrote something the other day, about the
grandeur of organic life's patience and
fortitude. I'm not sure I get it, exactly. But I
love hearing him go on about it.

MURIEL

Yes, exactly! Facing death, finally, Joe sees
life in all its terrifying immensity and
beautiful detail!

VERONICA

Wow. How am I going to tell my parents?

MURIEL

(embraces Veronica)
We must all be brave. But first we need to
get him to admit it.

VERONICA

Admit what?

MURIEL

That he's—that he's... Well, at least he's
got to open this envelope and tell us what's
going on.

VERONICA

I've never lost anyone before—no one close.

MURIEL

Loss enriches one, Veronica. It's sad but
true.
(removing costume)
Come! We must go to him now.

They move off in an explosion of flash photography.

26. EXTERIOR, ELIZABETH'S BUILDING

Joe comes down into the foyer and peeks out the door. He sees Mick and Keith across the street waiting for him to emerge. They pretend they're reading their text messages like detectives in an old movie hiding behind open newspapers. Joe steps out and the young men scatter. Just then, he hears...

                    CLARA
          Joe!

Looking over, he sees a woman in her mid-forties approaching.

                    JOE
          Clara.

                    CLARA
          Is your phone not working?

                    JOE
                (reaches for it)
          No, it's here.

                    CLARA
                (inspects)
          You have to turn it on.

She turns it on.

                    JOE
                (enlightened)
          Oh, wow. Is that... Okay.

They embrace.

                    CLARA
                (looks up at building)
          How's Elizabeth?

                    JOE
          Well.

CLARA
Are you heading back home?

JOE
Yes.

She links arms with him and they walk on.

CLARA
What did you need to discuss?

JOE
What are you expecting from me after I die?

She stops and looks at him.

CLARA
What's wrong? What are you talking about?

JOE
I'm fine. Laura is drawing up my will. I need
to decide what I'll leave to whom and all that.
It's called estate planning.

Clara thinks a moment then walks on.

CLARA
Nothing. You have no obligations. We're
divorced. I'm with someone else.

JOE
But you're still my best friend.

CLARA
What about Muriel?

JOE
She's everything else.

CLARA
And what does she expect?

Joe stops, sits on a park bench and thinks.

                    JOE
          It's hard to tell. She thinks much faster than
          I do. I think she wants to get married.

                    CLARA
          Really?

                    JOE
          Well, she wants to know if there's a future
          for us. She says she needs an anchor.

                    CLARA
          Do it!

                    JOE
          Really?

                    CLARA
          Don't you need an anchor too?

                    JOE
          Maybe. I don't know. But maybe not one
          outside myself.

                    CLARA
                    (takes his hand)
          Listen, your opportunities are not unlimited.
          You're almost sixty. Muriel is smart, hard-
          working, talented. She's rich and famous.
          She's very pretty—and you do like them
          pretty, you know. She's age-appropriate too
          —barely. I'd hate to see you making a fool of
          yourself in years to come running around after
          adorable fawns.
                    (adds, picturing it)
          Using a cane.

                    JOE
          She once famously said her work is her life.

CLARA

Just like you, twenty years ago.

JOE

(stung)

Yeah. I'm sorry. I neglected you.

CLARA

I should have known better. I was infatuated
with your activity, your achievements, your
reputation. But I only really came to know
and love you later, when I no longer depended
on you.

(then, remembers)

And what is all this about getting a job in the
graveyard!

JOE

I want to work outdoors, with my hands,
around nature. I want to be physically tired
when I get home in the evening.

CLARA

So, no more romantic comedies? The world
does need romance and comedy, you know.
And you're not bad at those.

He stands and paces, then stops.

JOE

Well, sure, if a project comes along. Anyway,
I'm not as in demand as I once was, you know.
Still, I feel I'm supposed to be working at—
working towards—something else.

CLARA

(skeptical)

Like what?

He looks around to make sure his response is not overheard, then
comes closer.

JOE
(quietly)
Peace, quiet, and reconciliation.

CLARA
(speechless, then)
You see, this is what happens when you allow
lawyers to talk you into making last wills and
testaments! You get all philosophical and
otherworldly!

JOE
It's not otherworldly, though. I just want to
know where to land—in this world.

CLARA
You should land wherever you are—on your
feet, wherever you find yourself.

JOE
Well, now I find myself in a place where—
where I'm interested in—well, in husbandry.

CLARA
(grabs his hand)
Right! So, marry Muriel!

JOE
No: Husbandry. Listen, I wrote it down.
(reads from notebook)
"Husbandry: the care, cultivation and management of natural resources."

CLARA
Such as?

JOE
Trees, hedges, grass and so on.

CLARA
In a cemetery?

JOE

It's close by. I don't want to leave the city.

She gives up, stands, and leads the way home.

CLARA

You're hopeless.

JOE

(follows)

Where did all that silverware in my kitchen drawer come from?

CLARA

Your father gave it to us when we got married.

JOE

Why didn't you take it when we split up?

CLARA

I was changing my life. Taking charge. Shedding my past. No time for fine silverware.

JOE

It's wasted on me.

CLARA

You don't need forks and knives?

They pause for a traffic light, they hold hands.

JOE

Yeah, but there's enough for, like, eight people.

CLARA

Exactly! You're not meant to be alone!

27. INTERIOR, JOE'S APARTMENT

Eric is in the studio with Joe's black Les Paul strapped on. He's plugged into the amp, shreds a little, and only then notices Joe and Clara.

ERIC
(of guitar)
I'll take this one if we're still friends when
you keel over and die.

JOE
How'd you get in here?

ERIC
I still have keys from last summer. Hey Clara!

CLARA
(in kitchen)
Eric, play something nice for a change: something peaceful, quiet and reconciling.
(opens drawer)
Ah! Here it is.

She lifts some pieces of their silverware. Meanwhile, Joe sits in
the studio with Eric and writes in his notebook.

JOE
"Black Les Paul goes to Eric."

ERIC
You gotta case for this, right?

JOE
Yeah. But I'll write that down so there's no
heartbreak or scandal.

ERIC
(sits back)
How long you planning on sticking around?

JOE
Me? My dad lived to be ninety, for thirty-
two years after he retired.

ERIC
(does the math)
So, he retired when he was our age.

JOE
After thirty years as a skilled union laborer
—with a pension.

ERIC
Jesus, that's a whole second life.

JOE
It's exciting to think a man—a man our age
—might turn and step away from his career,
his accomplishments, his professional
reputation even, and set his sights on other
things—at this age. Right?

CLARA
Don't listen to him, Eric!

Warned, they lower their voices.

JOE
Have you done your will?

ERIC
No. I should get on it, though.

JOE
I suppose you'd just leave everything to your
wife and daughter.

ERIC
"Everything?"

JOE
Something?

ERIC
There's not much to speak of.

JOE

There's the house.

ERIC

And the mortgage on the house.

JOE

Savings?

Eric sets aside the guitar and shrugs.

ERIC

The daughter has her eyes on graduate school.
So, there's another student loan on the horizon.

JOE

Oh yeah? What's she want to study?

ERIC

Post-Feminist Critical Theory and Gender
Studies—a degree in which will set her up
with a job as a cashier in a supermarket.

Someone is knocking at the door.

JOE
                (stands)
Hold on.

Joe opens the door and finds his neighbor, Tom Webster. The man
is clearly saddened and sympathetic.

JOE

Hey, Tom.

TOM

I heard the news. I had to come over.

JOE
                (enters kitchen)
What news? You want a beer?

                         TOM
                       (follows)
                 Yeah, thanks. Hey Eric.

                         JOE
              Tom, you know Clara, right?

Tom studies Clara sorting through Joe's forks and knives.

                         TOM
              I'm afraid not.

                        CLARA
              The ex-wife.

                         TOM
              I live across the hall.

                        CLARA
              Nice to meet you.
                    (then, to Joe)
              This all needs to be soaked in hot water and
              polished.

She carries the whole drawer of silverware down the hall to the
bathroom. Tom sits at the kitchen table, distraught.

                         TOM
              I understand you're preparing... That you're...
              I'm sorry. Preparing for the... for the end.

                         JOE
                       (puzzled)
              Who have you been talking to?

                         TOM
              I met your niece on the street.

                         JOE
                       (lightly)
              Yeah? And what did she say?

                          65

TOM

The will. The cemetery. I myself saw you in
church. Your ex-wife is absconding with the
silverware, for god's sake!

JOE

Tom, look, I'm perfectly fine.

TOM

You're being very brave about all this.

JOE

I'm just having my will made up. It's called
estate planning. You know, in case something
happens to me and... Someone's gotta know
what to do with all this stuff I've accumulated.

Joe heads back into the studio and starts cataloguing his music
library. Tom stands and follows.

TOM

So, you're not dying?

JOE

No.

TOM

What were you doing at the church?

JOE

Applying for a job in the graveyard.

Relieved, Tom sits down. They toast and drink.

TOM

Still, this gives you an opportunity to examine
your soul and make your peace with god.

JOE
(busy making notes)
I don't believe in god, Tom.

                    TOM
                  (impatient)
    Don't allow yourself to get tripped up by mere
    terminology. There's an underlying ground to
    all existence and you know it.

Joe is already down the hall by the bedroom.

                    JOE
                  (calls back)
        Do I know that?

                    TOM
        You've made films about it!

                    ERIC
                  (stops playing)
    You should talk to this lady professor who's
    writing a book about him!

                    TOM
        I'm sure she'd agree.

                    ERIC
    I don't think so. She's fairly convinced his
    entire body of work is a demonstration of the
    bad faith which typifies human relationships
    generally. But she thinks that's a good thing.

                    JOE
    Tom, you could use my library, couldn't you?

Tom stands and goes partway down the hall to look.

                    TOM
    What would I do with all that? My eyesight,
    you see. I can hardly make out my hand in
    front of my face anymore. Hey, you know,
    this beer ain't half bad.

There's a knock on the door.

JOE
(calls)
It's open!

Oliver enters.

OLIVER
Hey Eric.
(then)
Tom, you got hot water?

TOM
Not since yesterday.

OLIVER
Shit.

Oliver follows Joe into the kitchen.

OLIVER
So, what's this I hear: you're dying?

JOE
(nonplussed)
Wow, this is really getting out of hand.

Tom joins them, sits at the table, and continues the earlier conversation.

TOM
Anyway, many of your characters are religious.

OLIVER
(gets himself a beer)
Or they're struggling with religion as one
possible way of making sense of things. I agree.

The phone rings in the studio.

JOE
Excuse me.

                            TOM
                     (to Oliver, continuing)
Which may indicate, on his part, an ambivalence
tending towards belief.

                           OLIVER
Or a dissatisfaction with religious emotionalism.

                            JOE
                      (answers phone)
Hi. This is Joe.

28. INTERIOR, BAR

(Intercut with previous scene) Mick is on his mobile phone. He's
nervous and uncertain. Keith urges him on with stern looks and
emphatic gestures.

                           MICK
Mister Fulton?

                            JOE
Yes.

                           MICK
Mister Fulton, I think I'm your son.

                            JOE
What?

                           MICK
Or my friend, Keith, here, he thinks I might
be your son.

                           ERIC
                       (of phone call)
What's up?

                            JOE
                        (irritated)
Some punk saying he's my son.

OLIVER
(enters from kitchen)
You've got kids?

JOE
No.
(into phone)
Listen, stop calling this number. I don't have
a son.

And he hangs up. Meanwhile—

OLIVER
Eric, here, sign my petition.
(then, to Joe)
See, word gets around you're making your
will and dying...

JOE
I am not dying!

OLIVER
Whatever. They'll come out of the woodwork
hoping for part of the legacy. That's how the
unseen hand of a liberal economy operates.

ERIC
(to Oliver of apartment)
We're standing in Joe's legacy, hombre.
How big is this joint anyway?

OLIVER
The B-line? This is eight hundred and ten
square feet depending on the hallway variance.
(then)
Tom, come on, sign my petition.

Meanwhile, Joe is on the phone again. He dials, waits, then—

JOE
Laura? Yeah, it's Joe. Listen I just got a crank

call from some kid claiming to be my son.

29. INTERIOR, LAW OFFICE

Laura jumps up from her desk, furious.

LAURA
You see! This is what I'm talking about! I'll
be right over!

30. INTERIOR, JOE'S APARTMENT

Tom returns from the bodega with more beer. Joe, with Laura's list, is at the tiny kitchen table with Eric and Oliver.

JOE
I also have to state what I want done for my
funeral and how it's to be paid for.

OLIVER
You gotta leave some money for that too. A
capitalist scam to keep you in debt even after
you're dead!

JOE
What does that even cost?

TOM
Standard casket and wake type thing is about
ten thousand.

ERIC
At least.

Someone else is knocking at the door and Joe goes to answer it.

JOE
Well, I'm going to be cremated.

ERIC
They'll charge you for that, though, too.

OLIVER

They get you coming and going, man.

At the door, Joe finds Mick and Keith in the hallway.

MICK

Look, Mister Fulton, I really think I might be
your son.

JOE

Oh man!

KEITH
(lunges in)
You're Mick's biological dad! Admit it!

Joe grabs Keith by his shirt and slams him against the wall where
he slides to the floor, dazed.

JOE
(to Mick)
Go in the kitchen.

Mick steps over Keith and enters the kitchen just as Laura arrives.
She looks at Keith on the floor.

LAURA

That him?

JOE

That who?

LAURA

The pretender. The aggrieved plaintiff. Your
unknown son?

JOE
(lets her in)
No, he's in the kitchen.

Embarrassed, Mick sits at the kitchen table.

MICK

I just need an introduction to Muriel Hoffman,
honest.

LAURA

Is this blackmail?

MICK
(panics)
What? No! I just...

JOE

Settle down. Here, have a beer.

MICK
(of Extra Ultra Light)
Oh, hey. These are not so bad, right?

JOE

Who's your mom?

LAURA
(comes forward)
Joe, I'll handle this.
(sits)
Who's your mom?

MICK

Marta.

JOE
(stunned)
Marta?

LAURA
(to Joe)
Marta who?

JOE

You remember. That film in Stockholm. The
girl on the moped.

                    LAURA
With the tattoo?

                    MICK
Behind her right shoulder.

                    JOE
Pirate chick type thing—but quite explicit.

                    MICK
Exactly!

                    JOE
          (points)
She gave me that clock.

                    LAURA
          (scandalized, to Mick)
That's your mom?

                    MICK
Hey, lady, look, everyone's young once.

                    LAURA
          (takes notes)
Last name?

                    MICK
Bjorkman. Recently Chenowski. Though she's
since divorced.

                    LAURA
We can settle this out of court with a DNA
test, Joe. Though it will cost money.

                    JOE
          (to Mick)
Listen, you talk to her?

                    MICK
My mom?

                    74

JOE
Yeah. What did she say?

MICK
She thinks it's unlikely.

Keith staggers in from the hall.

KEITH
But still, man, you had intimate relations with
the guy's mom!

JOE
It was consensual.

KEITH
So what! And it was like before he was even
born. Still, you owe him something!

JOE
I owe *him* something?

MICK
I'm okay, actually.

KEITH
Mick, shut up!

JOE
Like what do I owe him?

KEITH
Like to introduce him to your girlfriend so he
can get her to read the miniseries he's written
for her!

JOE
Is that all?

MICK
It would be awesome.

JOE
(to Laura)
What do you think?

Laura stands, removes her coat and looks for the bathroom.

LAURA
Old-fashioned small-time extortion? I'm
all for it. Less expensive than litigation or
the DNA option.
(at bathroom)
Clara!

CLARA
Laura!

Meanwhile, back in the kitchen—

ERIC
You guys are named Mick and Keith?

KEITH
(threatened)
Yeah, so?

ERIC
Like the Stones?

KEITH
The who?

ERIC
No, the...
(waves it away)
Never mind.

Joe hands the young men cash and pushes them towards the door.

JOE
Look, run down to the bodega and get some
more of these Extra Ultra Lights.

31. INTERIOR, JOE'S BUILDING

Keith and Mick hustle across the lobby and tumble out onto the sidewalk, too excited to notice Leonard studying the apartment registry on the wall beside the entrance.

                    MICK
     There was a band called the Stones, I think.

                    KEITH
     Oh yeah! They did that song—

                    MICK
     About Jumping Jack Somebody or other—

                    KEITH
     A street fighting man—

                    MICK
     Exiled on Main Street and shattered.

                    KEITH
     My dad had that on vinyl. But I sold it to get
     this tattoo.

32. INTERIOR, JOE'S APARTMENT

The door is ajar. Leonard knocks, looks in, and enters. Joe and his friends look over and see him.

                    OLIVER
     Leonard!

                    LEONARD
     The door was open.

                    JOE
     Come on in.

                    LEONARD
     The church council decided to hire you. Can

you start Monday?

                    JOE
Sure!

                  LEONARD
Here, you gotta fill out these insurance papers.

                  OLIVER
Leonard, sign my petition.

                  LEONARD
What's it for?

                  OLIVER
              (hands him a pen)
I'm running for city council. Here, sign right
there.

                  LEONARD
Nice place you got here, Joe.
              (then)
Rodriguez, this pen don't work.

33. INTERIOR, BODEGA

Octavio wheels in a hand truck stacked high with six-packs of the
Extra Ultra Lights while Keith and Mick drag more of them out
from the cooler.

                    MICK
              (amazed)
I can't believe this is happening.

                  KEITH
            (heads for register)
Believe it. We played this perfectly. We're
gonna be rich, powerful, and influential!

But they stop, amazed to discover Muriel Hoffman is in the next
aisle advising Veronica.

MURIEL

But we can't be hysterical. We must be
supportive.

VERONICA

Supportive of Joe dying?

MURIEL

No, of his decision. He's clearly accepted his
death and is preparing for it in a very handsome
and graceful way. We don't want to interfere
with the dignity of this.
(searching)
Where is the cranberry juice?

VERONICA

Here it is.

They make their way to the register. Mick and Keith hang back,
stunned.

MICK

(remorseful)
So, Joe is dying!

KEITH

Look, he's not your father, after all.

MICK

Yeah, I mean, not literally. But, considering
all that's happening.

KEITH

What's happening is that you're about to meet
the actress who can get your television series
financed. Focus! Come on.
(of Veronica)
Who's the girl?

MICK

What girl?

At the register, Muriel pays. But before leaving, she stops and turns to Veronica.

> MURIEL
> Remember: no hysterics.

> VERONICA
> Right.

> MURIEL
> Calm, reasonable, but resolute.

> VERONICA
> Okay.

They leave just as Mick and Keith come up and stack their six-packs on the counter.

34. INTERIOR, JOE'S APARTMENT

In the bathroom, Clara is polishing the silverware while Laura peruses the bookshelves.

> LAURA
> Are we concerned that all Joe's philosophy
> books are in the bathroom?

> CLARA
> He's always liked to pursue the life of
> the mind close to the brute facts of nature.

Laura closes the toilet seat and sits there with a book.

> LAURA
> Yes, that would help keep things in
> perspective, I imagine.
> *(flips through pages, then)*
> Joe's not a terribly clever man, is he?

> CLARA
> No, but he's often inspired.

LAURA
Yes, and he's patient.

CLARA
Hardworking.

LAURA
I'm afraid I've billed him for more hours of
legal work than any other client in my career.

CLARA
Really?

LAURA
He trusts people so much. It's my job to
substantiate that trust. And it's not always so
easy.

CLARA
When he was a boy, they asked him what he
wanted to be when he grew up. He couldn't
decide and finally made a list: a carpenter, a
baseball player, a priest, or something that
would allow him to be all these things at once.

Laura stands and replaces the book on the shelf.

LAURA
You mean, like a director of romantic comedies?

CLARA
Apparently.

They hear the men laughing in the kitchen.

LAURA
My god—and these friends he makes!

35. INTERIOR, JOE'S APARTMENT

At the kitchen table—

TOM

You don't want a funeral?

JOE

No.

OLIVER

Not even a wake?

JOE

I'll leave money for a party.

LEONARD

Pizza and beer type thing?

JOE
(nods)
Exactly. No speeches.

OLIVER

Wow. Okay, hard core.

TOM

Joe, heaven has room even for those of
little faith.

JOE
(fascinated)
You have no doubts at all, huh?

TOM

About what?

JOE

Well, god, for instance.

TOM

How can I? Look at those trees out there.
The birds. The buildings. Those kids
playing in the street. My own hand. I'm
astonished constantly.

ERIC

So, you believe in hell too, I suppose?

But before Tom can answer this, they all look over to see Muriel in the kitchen doorway, pale and alarmed.

JOE

Muriel, you okay?

Muriel passes out and collapses in a spectacular and lovely fashion. Everyone jolts into action and Joe carries her into the bedroom. Mick and Keith arrive with the beer just in time to see Joe lay Muriel on the bed. Clara works the unconscious woman out of her coat. She checks her pulse and temperature.

CLARA

She'll be okay. She's just upset. No more talk
about last wills and testaments and graveyards!
(leaving)
I'll deal with this mob.

Clara ushers everyone out of the room and back to the kitchen; everyone except Veronica, who remains at Joe's shoulder. Joe kneels beside the bed and takes Muriel's hand. She revives.

JOE

Muriel.

MURIEL

I'll survive.

JOE

You'll survive what?

She leans up and touches his face.

MURIEL

There's no need to pretend for my sake.

JOE

I'm not pretending.

MURIEL

We have the letter.

JOE

What letter?

Muriel looks to Veronica.

VERONICA

From the hospital.

She hands it to Joe who opens it, reads, and hands it to Muriel.

JOE

It's a receipt for a donation I made. It's tax
deductible, apparently.

Muriel glances at the letter but is too worked up to see anything.
She hands it off to Veronica. The girl studies it, turns it over, then
drops it to the floor.

VERONICA

Then why didn't you just tell us! Uncle Joe,
you're so difficult!

And she storms out, slamming the door behind her.

MURIEL

You're really not dying?

JOE

No. But if you want me to, I will.

MURIEL

Don't say that.

JOE

Listen, Muriel, since I'm on my knees already:
will you be my wife?

She watches him, looks away, returns, kisses him on the mouth and then leans back.

                    MURIEL

No.

                     JOE

No? Really?

                    MURIEL

I'm sorry.

                     JOE
You no longer need an anchor?

                    MURIEL
Not one outside myself, no.

                     JOE
That's very brave of you.

                    MURIEL
                (graciously)
Thank you.

He gets to his feet and sits beside her on the bed.

                     JOE
May I continue to hope?

                    MURIEL
Of course. It will lend our lives urgency and
suspense.
                (stands)
Now, listen: I'm not going to do season fourteen
of *The Invincible Allura.*

                     JOE

Wow.

                    MURIEL
I'm done being a superhero.

JOE

Millions of viewers will be heartbroken.

MURIEL
(paces, concentrated)

Yes. I'll be replaced. Soon forgotten. They'll love somebody else.

JOE

But what now?

MURIEL

I don't know. Do you have any ideas?

JOE

There's a young hustler in the kitchen just now, a writer for television, your biggest fan in the tristate area. He's got a script about a Catholic nun.

MURIEL
(intrigued)

A nun?

JOE

The youthful mother superior of a convent in Brooklyn where they make beer to support their spiritual aims.

MURIEL

I like this.

36. INTERIOR, JOE'S APARTMENT

Later, in the kitchen, Muriel and Clara are reading lines from Mick's script. Laura, as prompter, follows along with a copy of her own. Mick and Keith watch excitedly.

CLARA
(reads)

Sisters!

MURIEL

(reads)

Ah! Sister Bernadette! Good morning.

CLARA

What's going on here!

MURIEL

We're building a brewery!

CLARA

You're what?!

MURIEL

We're going to make beer and market it to
support ourselves!

CLARA

(nearly faints)

Good God in heaven, what's to become of your
holy church on earth!

MURIEL

Sister Bernadette, I'm aware you are less than
happy with the bishop's appointment of me as
mother superior. But we must make the best
of it.

CLARA

I should never have agreed to this. You're not
mother superior material. You're—I'm sorry,
but—too charming. It's your, your sophistication,
your progressive views, your *joie de vivre*! Are
you wearing lipstick?

MURIEL

Sister, there are two parts to our vocation:
prayer and action.

CLARA

But prayer comes first.

Muriel poses dramatically, like a saint in a painting.

> MURIEL
>
> Maybe. But we cannot pray if we do not
> eat.

Everyone is impressed. Muriel throws aside the script and presses her hand to her chest.

> MURIEL
>
> I love it. It must be done.
> *(then, to Mick)*
> Of course, Joe should direct it, no?

> MICK
> *(astounded)*
> Would he?

> LAURA
>
> Terms will need to be negotiated, but I think
> it's likely.

> MURIEL
>
> And, of course, she will remain an activist.

> MICK
>
> Of course!

> MURIEL
>
> And get rid of the psychic powers thing.

> MICK
>
> Done.

> KEITH
> *(softly, to Mick)*
> You sure?

> MURIEL
>
> A vehement radical with deep and
> complicated passions.

MICK

I love it.

CLARA

Controversial.

LAURA

Wanted by the law!

MURIEL

Everywhere.

KEITH
(misunderstands)
Kinky! Competitive! Treacherous!

MURIEL

No, just idealistic. Unselfish.

CLARA

A real person with a conscience.

MURIEL

You know: common decency. That kind of
thing.

KEITH
(skeptical)
This could be hard to sell.

MICK
(already typing)
I'm sure we can make it work.

37. INTERIOR, JOE'S APARTMENT

Back in the bedroom, Joe continues to catalogue his possessions.
Veronica enters—

JOE
Veronica, you can take the books, right?

VERONICA
Uncle Joe, get real! This?
(of library)
This is a fire hazard.

Muriel and Laura enter, handing Joe Mick's script.

MURIEL
It's great. Will you direct it?

JOE
This thing about nuns?

MURIEL
Nuns who start a brewery!

LAURA
We can get this financed in a heartbeat,
Joe. Think about your pension plan.

Joe takes the script and wanders out of the room. As he moves toward the studio, flipping through the pages of the script, his friends all flood out from the kitchen. Oliver goes to the blackboard on the wall and lifts a piece of chalk.

OLIVER
No! I figured it out. If there's such a thing as
hell, it works like this—

Muriel rushes forward to stop him.

MURIEL
Wait! That's a work of art!

OLIVER
(of blackboard)
The blackboard?

MURIEL
It's by, oh, what's his name? He's terribly
famous.

TOM

He did that piece in the Whitney Biennial.

ERIC

With the car sawn in half and the raw meat.

VERONICA

Oh, yeah, he's married to that girl in the
movie about the rock star and the scientist.

MICK

Who get lost in the woods.

VERONICA

What's it called?

KEITH

It won awards and shit.

MICK

Whatever.

JOE

Oliver, please continue.

OLIVER

Desecrate the artwork?

JOE

Yeah, sure. It's only conceptual anyway.

OLIVER

I think it's like this: if there's a hell...
          (chalks "hell" on the board)
It's got to be the moment of death when you're
still cognizant enough to feel fear...
          (chalks this)
Regret...
          (chalks this)
And anger.
          (chalks this)

JOE
You just made this up?

OLIVER
No, I've been working on it in the evenings.

MURIEL
So, to avoid hell, one's moment of death
should be free from fear, regret and anger.

OLIVER
To die happily. That's the idea, yeah, because
those last moments, when you're helpless to
change anything, that's a... it's a... ah... Oh,
what do call it?

MURIEL
An eternal present.

OLIVER
That's it! An eternal present.

He adds that to the board as well and draws lines from one subject
to another, creating a diagram.

ERIC
(pensive, aside)
And that's gotta suck: lying there dying and
knowing you should have apologized to your
kid for being a jerk. Or that lie you told your
wife that you know she knows is a lie but she
hasn't said anything but you still feel like shit.

TOM
(concerned)
Hey, Eric, everything okay at home?

Leonard hits Keith lightly in the chest and points to the diagram.

LEONARD
So, you gotta live your life like that.

KEITH

Like what?

LEONARD

You gotta live so you don't do anything
you'll regret.

KEITH

Everyday?

LEONARD

Every moment of everyday.

KEITH

That's insane!

ERIC

Because you can die at any minute, see, and
you don't want to be angry or regretful in
those last moments and die uneasily.

OLIVER

Yeah, I think, basically, that's it. The eternal
present. Right there. I'm still working on it,
though. I got a three-dimensional model of it
down in the tool room.

Keith gets a new beer and sits at the kitchen table.

KEITH

You guys are nuts! Anger makes the world go
around. Everyone knows that. Competition.
Aggression. It's natural—the measure of a
person's worth. Regret: that's just the cost of
doing business. I say don't care about anything
or anyone and let other people look after their
own happiness.
         (to Veronica)
Am I right or am I right?

Preoccupied, Veronica looks up from her tablet.

VERONICA

Sorry. I was checking my e-mail. Excuse me.

And she leaves the room. Disappointed, Keith drinks his beer. But then he stands up and takes a picture of Oliver's diagram with his phone.

38. INTERIOR, JOE'S APARTMENT

In the studio, Joe is at his desk, already at work on Mick's script. Muriel glides in and switches on the desk lamp to help him. Then, leaning in and pointing to the page—

MURIEL

I'll need to play twenty-five at least some
of the time.

JOE

Easy.

She kisses him on the head and leaves. He pats himself down, looking for his glasses. Clara then materializes and places them on his face.

JOE

Thank you.

CLARA

The silverware is back in the drawer. You'll
need it. They've ordered food delivered.

She, too, kisses him fondly and moves off. Joe reads and lifts his pencil. He makes a note, then another. Finally, Veronica hurries in and sits beside him.

VERONICA

What was that lullaby you used to sing us
when we were little?

JOE

I sang lullabies?

VERONICA
It was like the saddest thing imaginable, but
we loved it. About a horse.

JOE
Oh, that! A song I heard somewhere.

VERONICA
Sleepy horses. Something, something...

JOE
(tries to recall)
Silent sunlight, welcome in.

VERONICA
Hold on.

She raises her tablet and prepares to dictate into it.

JOE
Silent sunlight...

VERONICA
(repeats into tablet)
Silent sunlight...

JOE
Welcome in...

VERONICA
Welcome in...

JOE
There is work we must now begin.

VERONICA
There is work we must now begin.

JOE
(can't remember)
Something, something, something.

VERONICA

Something, something, something.

JOE

Sleepy horses...

VERONICA

Sleepy horses!

JOE

Heave away...

VERONICA

Sleepy horses, heave away...

JOE & VERONICA
(half singing)

Put your backs to the golden hay / Don't ever
look behind at the work you've done...

VERONICA

For your work has just begun.

JOE

There'll be the evening in the end...

VERONICA

There'll be the evening in the end...

JOE

But till that time arrives...

VERONICA

But till that time arrives...

JOE

You can rest your eyes...

VERONICA

You can rest your eyes...

                    JOE
    And begin again.

                  VERONICA
    And begin again.

Joe looks from Veronica to the script and puts his reading glasses
back on.

                    JOE
    And begin again.

The End ~

Meanwhile

01 INTERIOR, WENDY'S APARTMENT—DAY

It's morning in a stylishly appointed Brooklyn loft. Forty-five-year-old Joe Fulton fixes the kitchen sink while a twenty-five-year-old fashion model, Wendy, flips through a magazine wearing just her underwear and Joe's hat. Once he's done with the sink, Joe stands up, tosses his wrench into his briefcase and puts on his jacket. Wendy comes over, cuddles, and slips two crisp one-hundred-dollar bills into his breast pocket. He smiles and tucks them back in beneath the waistband of her underwear at the small of her back.

02. EXTERIOR, BROOKLYN—DAY

Joe comes up the sidewalk working his cell phone and stops. He listens, expecting someone to pick up, but hears a warning beep and a sound like the phone has died. He sighs and drops the phone back into his pocket. He then tries to get cash from an ATM but is refused. Frustrated and confused, he walks on.

03. INTERIOR, BROOKLYN PHONE STORE—DAY

Joe displays his phone to the young woman behind the counter.

                    JOE
        I need to put more money on my phone.

                   PALLAVI
        Cash or credit?

Joe looks through his wallet. He has sixteen dollars. He slips out a credit card.

                    JOE
        Amex.

Pallavi takes the credit card and punches in some numbers at the terminal. She swipes the card, waits, then—

                   PALLAVI
                  (gently)
        There's a problem with the card.

JOE
(alarmed)
With the Amex?

PALLAVI
Sorry.

He flips through his wallet and gets another.

JOE
Try the Visa.

She goes through the motions with this card, too, and Joe watches, interested. Finally—

PALLAVI
No good.

JOE
Fuck.

PALLAVI
You can pay cash.

Joe considers this carefully. He looks back down into his wallet and counts through the sixteen dollars. Finally, he sighs and takes back his dud Visa card.

JOE
No. Thanks.

04. EXTERIOR, BROOKLYN BRIDGE—DAY

Back out on the street, making for the Brooklyn Bridge, Joe passes by a whole block of new apartment buildings under construction. He stops and studies the progress. Finally, he moves on and sets out across the bridge towards lower Manhattan. About a quarter of the way along, he stops to light himself a cigarette. But his lighter is not working either. He stops, exasperated, and notices an attractive, though oddly preoccupied, woman paused at the railing of the walkway. She is leaning out over the railing, trying to view the busy roadway beneath them. But she is also smoking, so Joe approaches.

                    JOE
        Gotta light?

The woman, Amelia, looks him over. She steps down from the railing and reaches into her pocket for her lighter. He comes closer and she lights his cigarette.

                    JOE
              (smokes, relaxes)
        What are you doing?

                  AMELIA
        I was just wondering what a person would
        actually have to do if they wanted to jump
        off the famous Brooklyn Bridge these days.

                    JOE
        You're not thinking of jumping, are you?

She just shrugs and looks down at her shoes.

                  AMELIA
        That's none of your business.

This worries him and he looks away. Amelia steps aside and looks back down at the traffic and the water beyond.

                  AMELIA
        From this height, certainly from the height at
        the middle of the bridge, a falling body would
        encounter the water as if the water were
        concrete.

                    JOE
        Most likely.

                  AMELIA
        Someone could probably just jump down
        from that ledge over there and shimmy along

one of those I-beams, out to the edge, before
anyone even noticed.

Joe drops the cigarette and grinds it out with his heel.

> JOE
> Walk with me over to Manhattan and let's get
> a coffee.

She doesn't respond at once. She continues studying the bridge's
structure. Joe waits. But, finally, she turns back to him.

> AMELIA
> People who jump from bridges don't drown.
> They're smashed to pieces by the water. Like
> getting hit by a car more like.
> > *(yawns, then)*
> Thank you, no. I'm headed in the other
> direction.

> JOE
> Fair enough.

> AMELIA
> Thanks, though.

> JOE
> You gotta cell phone?

> AMELIA
> Yeah.

> JOE
> Punch my number into it.

> AMELIA
> > *(smiles, entertained)*
> No.

> JOE
> I'm striking out bad, huh?

AMELIA
(kindly)

Sorry.

JOE

No sweat. But can I use your phone to make
a call?

She thinks it over then hands him her phone.

JOE

Thanks.

He takes the phone and steps aside. He dials, waits—someone
answers.

JOE

Miho? It's Joe. Yeah. I'm down here on the
bridge looking right at your apartment. Can
you see me?

He begins waving at the South Bridge Tower Complex at the
Manhattan end of the bridge. But then he stops, surprised to learn—

JOE

Shanghai? You're in Shanghai now?
(listens a moment, then)
Oh. No, I wanted to borrow that inflatable bed
you have. Wendy and I had a sort of—you
know. It's over, I guess. She wants to marry
Phil. You know, the attorney. No, I'm okay.
Don't bother. I was gonna stay with... What?
Well, yeah, if I could stay at your place a few
days that would be great. Can I get the keys
from Hal? Okay. No sweat. I have his number.
Thanks. Yeah. You too. Good luck with the
show!

JOE
(hands Amelia her phone)

Thanks.

AMELIA
Your friend lives in that building there?

JOE
Yeah. But she's in Shanghai and I have to go
all the way up to 157th Street and Riverside
Drive to get the keys from her husband.

AMELIA
Well, the day is still young.

JOE
It is.

She walks off towards Brooklyn, turning back with a little wave.

AMELIA
See ya.

JOE
I hope so.

He watches her go, then starts off towards Manhattan.

05. EXTERIOR, FINANCIAL DISTRICT—DAY

Joe comes across a street in lower Manhattan, full of purpose and
resolve. He enters a bank.

06. INTERIOR, BANK—DAY

Joe is seated with the bank branch manager who is busy logging
into her computer.

ILIANA
Let me check.

JOE
(irritated)
There is at least three thousand dollars in the
account.

                    ILIANA
And you pay the Amex bill from this account?

                     JOE
Automatically each month.

She types, searches, and spots something unusual.

                   ILIANA
Oh, I see.

                     JOE
I can't even get money out of an ATM.

                   ILIANA
              (gravely)
Your assets have been frozen.

                     JOE
              (stunned)
What?

                   ILIANA
The State of New York has frozen all your
accounts.

For a moment, Joe is speechless. He sits forward.

                     JOE
Why?

                   ILIANA
              (carefully)
I don't know. Did you pay your taxes?

                     JOE
Yeah.
              (then, less certain)
I think.
              (then, convinced)
No, of course, I did. I paid my taxes.

ILIANA

Yes, here it is: an amount paid to New York
State Department of Finance.

JOE

One thousand seven hundred and six dollars.

ILIANA

On April 7th.

JOE

That sounds about right.

Iliana sits back away from the computer, helpless, and looks at him.

ILIANA

I'm sorry, Mister Fulton. But you've got to
talk to the New York State Department of
Taxation and Finance.

07. EXTERIOR, FINANCIAL DISTRICT— DAY

Joe storms across the street, dodging traffic.

08. INTERIOR, BROKERAGE HOUSE—DAY

It's a large corporate financial industry office. Joe's friend, Mike,
listens as Joe describes his plan.

JOE

Windows. Modern standard windows that are
used all over Europe. But the ones I think are
best are manufactured in Germany. I sent you
the names, right? You got those?

MIKE

Yes, right here. And how are they different?

JOE

They're more energy efficient. They let in
more light. They're less easy to break in

through. They're more attractive. All that
stuff. But the energy efficiency is, I think,
the real selling point.

Joe paces around the office while Mike thinks this through.

                    MIKE
And you want to import these windows to
the States?

                    JOE
All I need to do first is make a deal with this
contractor—Sullivan, Powers, Flynn—who'll
be building all those new condos over in
Brooklyn.
          (comes to Mike's desk)
Google the New York State Department of
Taxation and Finance.

                    MIKE
          (typing)
What have they got to do with this?

                    JOE
Nothing. The fuckers have frozen my assets
for some mysterious reason.

Mike locates the information and stands, offering Joe his desk.

                    MIKE
There it is.

Joe sits and copies down a phone number from off the computer
screen. He rolls the desk chair over to the phone and begins dialing
as he continues to explain.

                    JOE
At least two of those condos in Williamsburg
were designed by firms in Sweden. The
dimensions are right. Standard European
windows will fit perfectly. I just need the

capital to buy the windows and to get them
over here. Then, after we make some money
from these first couple of building projects,
we can order the Germans to make these
windows to scale for conventional American
home construction. Pretty soon the federal
government's sure to be offering tax incentives
for ecologically friendly manufacturing and
so on. Hold on.
>   *(into phone)*
English.
>   *(waits, then)*
Other.
>   *(waits, then)*
071-52-9189.

Mike steps away to give Joe privacy.

>   MIKE
> You want a coffee?

>   JOE
> Yeah, thanks.

Joe continues waiting. Finally, in response to another option, he
answers with a frown—

>   JOE
> Penalties.

He waits as he is redirected. Finally, an actual human being picks
up the line.

>   JOE
> Hello. Yes.
>   *(listens, then)*
> My assets have been frozen. I don't know.
> I filed on time and paid what I owed.
>   *(surprised)*
> For 2005? I under paid in 2005? How much?
> Two hundred dollars. Well, I don't recall

receiving a notice. It was four years ago.
What address have you got on file?
>   *(hearing the answer, he nods*
>   *and understands the problem)*

East 76th Street! Fuck...
>   *(rushes to apologize)*

No, sorry. It's just... Well, how can I pay you
when you've frozen my bank account?
>   *(it's explained, he takes notes)*

Yeah. So, it's two hundred I under paid and...
>   *(stunned)*

Fifteen hundred dollars in penalties!
>   *(stands, catches his breath)*

No, right away. Fax the form to...
>   *(reads Mike's business card)*

212-647-8230.
>   *(listens to further instructions)*

Once you have the signed form, you can take
the money? Okay. Yeah. And when will my
account be unfrozen? Tomorrow. Okay.

And he hangs up.

09. EXTERIOR, FINANCIAL DISTRICT—DAY

Joe and Mike walk along through the crowded streets.

MIKE
I'll call you later in the day. These guys could
move on something like this.

JOE
Okay.

MIKE
You've got a face-to-face relationship with
the German manufacturer?

JOE
Yeah. Heinrich. And he's very positive about
this.

MIKE

What about the contractor?

JOE

I've only had one phone call, but I'm tight
with the Swedish architects and they can force
it through.

MIKE

We'll need a business plan right away, though.

JOE

No problem. It's all in my head.

Amused and impressed, Mike stops at the corner.

MIKE

I thought you were a drummer.

JOE

I *am* a drummer.

They shake hands and Mike goes on his way. Joe looks around and
spots a deli.

10. INTERIOR, DELI—DAY

It's a busy little place with a sullen teenage girl at the register. Joe
removes a dollar bill from his wallet.

JOE

Can I get some quarters for the pay phone?

CASHIER

You gotta buy something.

JOE

Come on.

CASHIER

Those is the rules.

Joe grabs a six-ounce bottle of water and puts it on the counter.

CASHIER

Two dollars.

JOE

Are you kiddin' me?

She just waits with attitude. He replaces his single and pays with a five.

CASHIER

How many quarters?

JOE

Four.

11. EXTERIOR, FINANCIAL DISTRICT—DAY

Joe steps up to a payphone, drops in a couple of coins, and dials.

JOE

Hal? Yeah, Joe. Can I come get the keys to
Miho's place? She call you? Yeah. Between
three-thirty and five. Ok. I got some things to
do downtown first anyway. Yeah, we can talk
about that later. I'm seeing Nathalie this
afternoon. Okay. What's the cleaning lady's
name? Consuela. Right. Thanks.

He hangs up, drinks his expensive water, and watches as a Black African delivery man negotiates the narrow and crowded sidewalk with a hand trunk stacked high with a dangerous and unwieldy pile of deliveries. Joe makes room for him to pass and the man stops.

OTIS
(heavy accent)
Where is Bayard Street?

JOE

Bayard? In Chinatown?

                    OTIS
Bayard and Mott.

                    JOE
That's in Chinatown.

                    OTIS
Near here?

                    JOE
No. It's like fifteen blocks away.

                    OTIS
Which way? How?

                    JOE
You're gonna push this stuff all the way to
Bayard and Mott?

                    OTIS
No place to park around here.

                    JOE
Your truck's up in Chinatown, then?

                    OTIS
Bayard Street.

Joe circles the pile of deliveries and gauges the density of pedes-
trian and automobile traffic around them.

                    JOE
Dude, you can't push this thing all the way
to Chinatown.

                    OTIS
My truck is on Bayard Street.

                    JOE
Leave the stuff here with me and go get your
truck. You can load it up here in a minute and

be off. I've got an hour to kill.

                    OTIS
I do not know how to get to Bayard Street.

                    JOE
I'll tell you how. It'll take you half an hour at
most to walk there and drive back.

                    OTIS
Too much traffic. Too many streets. All one
way.

There is no way to argue with him. So, Joe guides Otis all the way
to Chinatown. They make their way out of the financial district,
they pass through the city government area, Joe out front, in traffic,
running interference so Otis doesn't get run over. They finally
locate the truck on Bayard Street and cross to it.

12. EXTERIOR, OTIS' TRUCK—DAY

Otis drives Joe north on the FDR highway. Joe leans over and tunes
the radio to the local news. He's worried to hear—

                CORRESPONDENT
                   (on radio)
The Coast Guard point out that the tide is
moving fast and the body of whoever jumped
has been carried far out into the harbor by
now. We expect no new information for at
least a few hours. Once again: numerous
people have notified the New York City police
that an unidentified person climbed out over
the Brooklyn bound lanes of the Brooklyn
Bridge at approximately ten-fifteen this
morning and leapt to what we believe is their
death in the East River. From the Brooklyn
Bridge, this is Maria Ramos for New York
One. Back to you, Chet.

Joe is startled. He turns and leans out the passenger side window, looking back at the Brooklyn Bridge half a mile behind them.

13. EXTERIOR, CHELSEA—DAY

Otis steers the van towards the westside, coming to a stop on 8th Avenue. Joe climbs out at the curb and comes around to the driver's side window.

> OTIS
> So, it goes: *el baño*?

> JOE
> *Dónde está el baño.*

> OTIS
> *Dónde está.*

> JOE
> Just say *el baño*. The bathroom. Everyone knows.

Otis nods and drives off. Joe looks up and down the street, then heads off towards a particular address. But he passes a desperate looking young girl he thinks he might know and slows down. She, too, slows down and finally stops, recognizing him.

> LORI
> You!

> JOE
> Lori, right?

> LORI
> You owe me money!

> JOE
> I owe *you* money?

> LORI
> For that commercial video thing last month. I was one of the models. And I didn't get paid!

JOE

Okay, now I remember.

LORI

I didn't get paid, you asshole!

JOE

Hey, calm down. What do you mean you
didn't get paid? Did you fill out an invoice
and give it to what's his name the production
manager?

LORI

Jason. Yeah. Of course. And I'm still waiting
for my check!

JOE

There must have been a mistake. I'll look
into it.

LORI

(starts to cry)

Pay me now!

JOE

I can't pay you now.

LORI

I really need money. I don't have anything.
And... and...

JOE

Here, sit down.

He ushers her over to sit on the doorstep of a building. He finds
some tissues in his briefcase and hands them to her.

JOE

Look, there's been a mix-up is all. We'll deal
with it. Where are you staying? Where do you
live?

LORI

I'm staying with some people I met. In the—
near Chinatown, I think.

JOE

You mean you moved?

LORI

Yeah.

JOE

What address did you put on the invoice?

She thinks this through and realizes she has made a mistake. She
hangs her head, angry and embarrassed.

LORI

I don't know. I guess. Shit. The old one.

JOE

Okay. Problem solved!

But she is furious with herself.

LORI

Fuck!

JOE

Easy.

LORI
(doubles over and moans)
I'm just so—I oughta just do everybody a
favor and kill myself.

JOE
(stern)
Hey, shut up!

She straightens up, startled. Joe's busy pacing and thinking. She
looks aside, ashamed.

                              LORI

          I'm hungry.

                              JOE

          Okay. Okay. Understood. Just no more of
          this fucking drama.

He drags out his wallet and considers the cash remaining. He's got
thirteen dollars; a ten and three singles. He takes out the ten and
hands it to her.

                              JOE

          Look, this is all I have right now.

                              LORI

          Are you kidding me!

                              JOE

          It's all I've got. Give me a number. I'll track
          down your money and get it to you.

                              LORI
                        (of her phone)
          I'm out of minutes!

Joe takes out his memo pad and writes.

                              JOE

          Listen.
                       (sits beside her)
          Tomorrow at nine o'clock in the morning be
          at this address and I'll pay you what I owe
          you. The corner of Broad and Stone Streets.

She studies the scrap of paper he hands her.

                              LORI

          Where is this?

                              JOE
          Near South Ferry. The Financial District. Ask

people the way. It's easy. There's a pizzeria
on the corner and an ATM right outside. I'll
be there. I'll have your money. Okay?

She broods a little longer and then tucks the slip of paper into her
pocket.

                         JOE
                    (repeats)
          Okay?

                         LORI
          Okay.

He takes out his wallet again and gives her his remaining three dollars. She accepts them.

                         JOE
                  (stands to walk off)
          Nine o'clock.

                         LORI
                    (grudgingly)
          Okay.

14. INTERIOR, REHEARSAL STUDIO—DAY

Joe enters and shakes hands with the members of a sophisticated
jazz folk quartet and approaches the drum set. He clicks open his
briefcase and removes his drum sticks. A little later, he auditions.
While he plays the simple, tasteful accompaniment to the standup
bass, guitar, and piano, he can't help but study the clothes the other
guys are wearing. They are impeccably dressed. The song finishes
and the band seems impressed with Joe's playing. But they look
him over as if it's all about the clothes. Joe is dressed pretty cool
too, but now he's a little self-conscious. The band leader glances at
Joe's resume.

                       CHARLES
                  (mildly impressed)
          You toured with Vince Capo?

JOE
(stands up from drums)
Yeah. Seven shows in Stockholm this past
spring. Berlin, Prague... The usual short tour.

Joe spots the bass player assessing the merits of his—Joe's—
shoes.

CHARLES
(sets aside resume)
Okay. We've got a few more people to see.
Thanks for coming in.

Joe nods graciously, tosses his drumsticks back into the briefcase,
and leaves.

15. EXTERIOR, CHELSEA—DAY

Joe comes out of the building, not optimistic. He pauses, looks
around, then walks away. He reaches the entrance of the nearest
subway station and pauses, still irritated. Two sharply dressed
teenage girls waiting to cross the street are watching him.

JOE
(steps closer)
You think these shoes go okay with this suit?

The girls look him over and consider. They nod affirmatively. The
shoes are okay. Joe nods, agreeing.

JOE
I thought so. Thanks.

He skips confidently down the steps to the subway. But down
below, he discovers his prepaid Metro Card doesn't work when he
swipes it at the turnstile. He looks around in disbelief and notices
there is no one working in the booth. He considers jumping the
turnstile, but doesn't. He reaches down into his pocket and sees he
has only two quarters left. Amazed, he heads back up to the street,
passing a young, homeless, college-aged kid sitting on the top step
with a sign reading *Over Qualified*. Joe drops his quarters into the

kid's cup.

16. EXTERIOR, MIDTOWN—DAY

Joe makes his way up Broadway, through Times Square, and finds himself before an office building he seems to know well. He hesitates, conflicted, but then enters.

17. INTERIOR, OFFICES—DAY

Joe's older brother, Jim, is a laidback middle management executive returning from a meeting. As he approaches, his secretary, Clair, announces—

> CLAIR
> Your brother's here.

Jim stops, surprised. He enters his office and finds Joe seated on the little couch inside.

> JIM
> Hey.

> JOE
> Hey.

Jim sits behind his desk.

> JIM
> What's going on?

> JOE
> I was just passing by and had some time. I'm on my way up to see Nathalie. Thought I'd stop in to see you too.

> JIM
> You okay? You need money?

Joe takes this little blow stoically and changes his mind about why he's there.

                              JOE
                No. I'm fine. Things are good. Busy.

Jim is gazing wistfully out at all the activity beyond his office door.

                              JIM
                God, I wish I had your life.

                              JOE
                Get outta here! What do you call all this?

Jim stands and looks out over the vast open-plan office space filled
with busy, cool, softly spoken employees busy with unknown purpose.

                              JIM
                I don't know. What *do* you call this?

                              JOE
                You've been here for twenty years, dude.

                              JIM
                        (turns back in)
                I don't even know what we do here anymore.
                I know it used to be about manufacturing
                parts for xerox machines but now it's all
                about some sort of photo-optimized computer
                chip for cell phones. Everyone in charge is
                half my age. I won't be here for long.

                              JOE
                How are the kids?

                              JIM
                Expensive.

                              JOE
                And Maureen?

                              JIM
                Less expensive, but difficult. Now that the

kids are in high school and don't need her
anymore, she says, she wants to move out
and join an Ashram. The yogi's pretty
famous. It's all about breathing, apparently.
The world will be saved through breathing.
                    (then, excited)
Hey! Did you produce that movie by what's
his name yet? *The Stations of the Cross* or
whatever?

                    JOE
No. Not yet. Mostly just these advertising
videos for an online marketer. The real thing,
though—the *real* thing has to do with windows.

                    JIM
                    (fascinated)
Windows?

                    JOE
Importing windows from Europe for use in
green technology building projects.

                    JIM
                    (impressed, but surprised)
Wow. This is unlike you.

                    JOE
Is it? No, this is me.
                    (reconsiders)
I guess.
                    (thinks and decides)
Yeah, no. It is me.
                    (finally, excited)
If this goes down, it'll be big.

                    JIM
What's involved?

                    JOE
An equity investment group in Ohio my

friend Mike is pitching it to. I'll know more
tomorrow or later today.

                    JIM
              (laughs)
You're amazing!

Joe enjoys his brother's enthusiasm. He stands and gets ready to
go, adding modestly—

                    JOE
Well, let's see what happens.

Jim walks him to the door.

                    JIM
         It'll happen. You sure you don't need any
         money?

Joe stops, controls his irritation, and looks at his brother.

                    JOE
         Hey, what? Do I look in a bad way?

                    JIM
         No. It's just I haven't seen you in like nine
         months and that was the outfit you were
         wearing then.

Joe steps back and displays himself.

                    JOE
              (defiantly)
         This is my look. I had a gig in Brooklyn last
         night. This is my look.

                    JIM
              (having ideas)
         Listen, if this window import thing goes
         down, let me know. I might need a job and
         I'm a manager. It's what I do.

This gives Joe pause. He looks aside and tilts back his hat as Clair enters with a folder.

                    JOE
          That's a good idea.

                    JIM
          Right? Clair, I'm a manager, right?

                    CLAIR
          He's a manager, that's true. I'm his secretary.
                    (to Jim, of folder)
          They want you to review this.

                    JOE
          Okay, brother, I'll be in touch!

Jim watches him go then wanders back to his desk, opens the folder and looks at the documents therein.

18. EXTERIOR, LINCOLN CENTER—DAY

Joe comes up Broadway from his brother's office, stops, and smacks himself in the back of the head, furious. He removes his wallet and just looks into its emptiness. He sits on a park bench out in front of the Opera House and searches his hat for hidden resources. Then he opens his briefcase and searches through all its secret places. But he finds nothing. He stands and walks on.

19. INTERIOR, BAR—DAY

Joe comes in from the sidewalk and stops. The place is almost completely empty, except for an older man, Paul, who sits at the end of the bar, clutching an old case of some kind on his lap as he nurses a whiskey. Joe nods respectfully and moves further up the bar. The bartender approaches, an attractive woman whose mood darkens when she sees Joe.

                    LIA
                    (scowls)
          What are you doing here?

JOE

I thought you wouldn't be working.
(checks his wristwatch)
It's Wednesday, right?

LIA

(eases up)
Chuck was in a car accident. I'm filling in.

JOE

He okay?

LIA

Yeah. Just hurt his elbow. He'll be back by
the weekend.

JOE

Look, I'm sorry, I didn't...

She cuts him off with a wave of her hand and sighs.

LIA

Never mind.
(offers him the phone)
Here, wanna call my little sister?

JOE

Look, I'll just leave then.

LIA

Stop. I'm sorry. Not really. But anyway.

JOE

(sits back down)
She came on to me. And you were off on
vacation with the well-dressed real estate
mogul.

LIA

Hey! That was not hanky-panky. I was trying
to get a job.

JOE

And besides, you and me never had any kind
of permanent thing. What the fuck is the
problem?

LIA

She's half your age!

JOE

That was not a problem for her.

Lia glances over at Paul. He looks away. She returns to Joe.

LIA

What are you drinking?

JOE

I just came in to sit down.

LIA

What?

JOE

I gotta walk all the way up to 157th Street.

LIA
(sarcastically)
To borrow money?

JOE

To get some keys.

LIA

Typical.

She pours him a glass of water and walks away. He drinks it grate-
fully. Then he looks again at Paul down at the end of the bar. Paul
is also watching Joe, clutching the old case to himself.

PAUL

Armand?

                    JOE

Excuse me?

                    PAUL

Are you Armand?

                    JOE

No.

                    PAUL

Sorry.

And he looks away. But Joe watches the man a moment longer. He
drinks his water and then, politely, ventures—

                    JOE
Excuse me, you're the author, right? The
novelist?

                    PAUL
                 (shyly)
Yes, I am.
                    JOE
              (raises his glass)
Cheers. I like your books.

                    PAUL

Thank you.

Noticing how Paul clutches the case in his arms while looking
anxiously towards the entrance, Joe asks—

                    JOE
Is everything okay?

                    PAUL
My typewriter is broken.

                    JOE
                 (of case)
That your typewriter?

PAUL

Yes.

JOE

I didn't think they still made them.

PAUL
(relaxes)
They don't. But there is a man, Armand, who
still fixes them or, to be precise, his son, also
named Armand, who fixes them. Armand the
elder died, I guess. He's fixed it before. But I
always had to mail it to this address and it
would come back, repaired, a week or two
later. I called the old number and an answering
machine instructed me to deliver the machine
personally to this address between noon and
2pm on Wednesdays.

JOE
(checks his wristwatch)
You been waiting here all that time?

PAUL

Yes.

Joe comes down the bar.

JOE

Let me take a look at it. You mind?

Paul hesitates, but then lifts the case up on to the bar. Joe opens it.
He is immediately impressed with the beauty of the machine and
leans back.

JOE

Oh! Nice!

PAUL
(intrigued)
You like machines, I see.

JOE

What's the problem in here?

PAUL

The keys jam.

JOE

It's rust. And metal shavings all mucked up
with, well: dust, dandruff, cigarette ash.

PAUL

That sounds like me.

JOE

Lia, you got a lemon?

Lia rolls her eyes, aggrieved, and obliges. She grabs a lemon and
wings it fiercely right at Joe's face. But he catches it deftly in one
hand.

PAUL

(amused)
A beautiful woman in a bad mood. You could
write a book about it.

JOE

You have. A few times, right?

PAUL

Yes. It's sort of my subject.

Opening the briefcase, Joe grabs his Swiss Army knife and a set of
miniature screwdrivers. Paul is intrigued and looks on as Joe slices
the lemon and squeezes it over the clot of stuck hammers in the
typewriter. Using the knife blade, he scrapes away at the shafts. He
loosens some screws, puffs away dried ink, and jiggles the stuck
mechanism.

JOE

The acid in the lemon juice loosens the grime.
That's all it is.

Then he reaches back into his briefcase and pulls out a small can of WD-40. Paul is terribly curious now about this briefcase.

> JOE
> WD-40, fixes everything. I always need it for the drum kit.

> PAUL
> Ah, so you're a drummer.

> JOE
> That too. Different things. I acted in a movie once but it never got distributed. I wrote a novel that was almost published. I might produce a movie. Recently, I make video content for an online ad agency and I'm trying to get this import business started— construction material, windows particularly.

He reaches over the bar and grabs the handheld vacuum. Tilting the typewriter upside down, he shakes it free of detritus and shoves the nozzle of the vacuum up inside the machine to suck up the excess. Done, he sets aside the vacuum and places the typewriter back in front of the famous author. Paul feeds in a sheet of paper and types a little. He sits back and smiles.

> PAUL
> Perfect, thank you.

> JOE
> Yeah? You sure?

> PAUL
> Let me pay you something.

> JOE
> No.

> PAUL
> But I would have paid Armand junior two hundred dollars!

JOE

No. Thanks. No.

PAUL

At least let me buy you a drink.

JOE

Okay.
            (calls)
Lia, a Jameson's on the rocks with a beer
chaser.

PAUL

Same here!
            (places typewriter aside)
What's your novel about?

Joe is not prepared for this. He puts his tools away and shrugs.

JOE

Love. Jealousy. Regret. Compassion.

PAUL

A tragedy.

JOE

You think so?

PAUL

Well, a comedy is supposed to end better
than it began. A tragedy worse.

JOE

But life is never that clear cut, is it?

PAUL

"Tragedy elevates us through sorrow and
comedy makes us forget." I think that's how
it goes. But forgetting is sad. And the comic
flaws of the elevated are easier to see, simply
because they're elevated.

Their drinks arrive. They toast.

> JOE
>
> Life gets you coming and going.
> *(they drink, then)*
> I wrote about a man who doesn't love anyone
> or anything anymore than he loves anyone else
> or any other thing.

> PAUL
>
> Very existentialist.

> JOE
>
> Maybe.

> PAUL
>
> Interior, I imagine. Not much action.

> JOE
>
> No one makes it to page twenty.

> PAUL
>
> Novelist, drummer, actor, movie producer,
> entrepreneur, typewriter repair man—you've
> got a lot on your plate.

> JOE
>
> It's harder to hit a moving target.

But Paul is not fooled by this self-effacement. He persists.

> PAUL
>
> I'm curious: what drives you?

> JOE
>
> You mean psychological motivation?

> PAUL
> *(laughs)*
> Sorry. Characters are my business. I'm
> interested professionally.

Joe gives it some thought. Finally—

> JOE

Success.

> PAUL
> Really? Worldly success?

> JOE

Yeah.

> PAUL

That's all?

> JOE
> I'd settle for that. Of course, sure, if an
> opportunity for some artistic or spiritual
> transcendence presented itself, I'd go for that
> too. As long as I didn't, you know, have to
> make a fool of myself.

> PAUL

A skeptic.

> JOE
> I keep thinking that if I had some sort of
> definite success at something, on the other
> side of that success there'd be a little more
> air to breath, more space, a minute would
> have sixty-three seconds.

> PAUL

And a mystic.

> JOE
> Ah, it's only the whiskey talking.
> *(but still, rattled)*
> I think a man gets a smell about him at a
> certain point: the unsuccessful smell. The
> odor of failure. And he's got to beat that.
> Outrun it.

(stands off the bar and shrugs)
Or just accept it, I guess. Live without such
expectations. I've read in books that there is
such a thing as the quiet, happy, and
uneventful life.
(then, of Paul)
But you might not—I mean no offense—you
might not know about this. You had your first
big success in, what, your twenties?

PAUL
(sips his whiskey)
Thirty-two. But it didn't last long. Thirty
years later, I'm still milking it.

JOE
Still, you had it. Something to build on. Some
concrete success.

PAUL
(wistful)
I'd like to do something different, though.

JOE
Can't you?

PAUL
I'm afraid.

JOE
Really?

PAUL
People like what they know. To change, to
explore—it's a risky business.

JOE
But you're *you.*

PAUL
I might not be me if I did something new. In

fact, even worse, I might be me, but in ruins.
> *(studies his whiskey)*

I admit it. I lack the courage to challenge the
world that way again.
> *(finishes drink)*

Can I give you a ride somewhere? I have a car
waiting outside.

20. EXTERIOR, EAST 76TH STREET—DAY

Paul's Driver pulls up at the curb. Joe steps out and the author gets
out with him, handing him a business card.

> PAUL

Send me your book.

> JOE
> *(surprised)*

Really?

> PAUL

Sure.

> JOE

I'm told it's really bad.

> PAUL

That's alright. I've read all the really good
books.

> JOE

Okay. I will.
> *(they shake hands)*
Thanks for the ride.

> PAUL

Take care, my friend.

Paul gets back in and the car drives off. Joe crosses the street to an
address he knows well. He buzzes a certain apartment. After a
moment, a woman's voice comes through the intercom—

NATHALIE
(off)
Hello?

JOE
Nathalie, it's me, Joe.

NATHALIE
Oh! Wow. Hey!

But she fails to buzz him in. Joe rolls his eyes, impatient.

JOE
Nathalie?

NATHALIE
Yeah?

JOE
You gonna let me in?

NATHALIE
(remembers)
Oh, right! Okay. Hold on.

The buzzer sounds and the lock is opened. He enters.

21. INTERIOR, NATHALIE'S APARTMENT—DAY

Nathalie is a beautiful 35-year-old actress. Half clad, she flurries around the apartment making herself presentable while still remaining essentially naked. There's a knock on the door. She tosses her hair around and drops into character.

JOE
(off)
Nathalie!

NATHALIE
(as if surprised)
Joe?

JOE

Open the door!

She undoes the bolt and welcomes him in, pretending to be deeply preoccupied.

NATHALIE

I was just rehearsing my lines.

The first thing Joe sees is a small, neat stack of letters from the New York State Department of Taxation and Finance lying on the entry-way table. He sorts through them.

JOE

Were you ever gonna tell me about this mail that was coming for me?

NATHALIE

Oh, I gathered you knew all about it and thought it unimportant.

JOE

And, so, you saved them all, nice and neat like, here on the table since 2005?

NATHALIE

Hey! You should have formally notified the New York State Department of Taxation and Finance about your change of address.

She spins on her heel dramatically and floats away into the next room. Joe enters the kitchen.

JOE
(calls)
What are you working on?

NATHALIE
(blasé)
Law & Order. I'm a semi-regular recurring role now.

JOE
(opens fridge)
Good for you. You gotta a coke or something
in here?

NATHALIE
Of course not! Have a cup of yogurt.

He finds a bottle of Heineken beer and lifts it.

JOE
(smirks)
Who's the man in your life who drinks
Heineken?

NATHALIE
Oh, that was... I don't know. A long time ago.

Joe opens the beer and drinks. He closes the fridge and comes to sit
beside her on the couch.

JOE
You look good, Nathalie.

NATHALIE
Oh, I haven't even, you know... I just woke
up and all. How's your project coming along?

JOE
Which project is that?

NATHALIE
The movie. *The Stations of the Cross.* Jesus!
The crucifixion! So dramatic!

JOE
Yeah, well, I need to talk to you about that.

NATHALIE
I'm still interested, you know, in the role of
Mary Magdalene. I'd love to play Jesus' lover.

140

Who wouldn't? I'm sure *Law & Order* would
give me time off.

                    JOE
The director knows who you are. And he likes
you.

                  NATHALIE

Really?

                    JOE
Yeah, well, but the thing is, he thinks you'd
be better cast in the role of the other Mary.

                  NATHALIE
                  (wary)
The other Mary?

                    JOE

Yeah.

                  NATHALIE
What other Mary?

                    JOE
The Virgin Mary.

The color drains from her Nathalie's and she stands up from the
couch, furious.

                  NATHALIE
He wants me to play Jesus' mother?

                    JOE
              (diplomatically)
A saint amongst women, apparently.

                  NATHALIE
              (throws a tantrum)
Fuck you! Get outta here! You scumbag! I
can pass for twenty-three and no one would

even blink! You tell Mister Director to just
go jump in a lake and die! Fucking moron!
Who the fuck does he think he is! I'm a
semi-regular-recurring role on one of the
most-watched crime dramas on American
television! Asshole! Get outta here! You
know the way!

She storms out onto the balcony. Joe drinks his beer, sets it down,
and picks up his old mail. There, to the side of the mail, is
Nathalie's purse. He opens it and sees a lot of cash. He takes two
twenty dollar bills and sets the purse back down. Then he goes out
to the balcony to see how she is.

JOE

Hey.

NATHALIE
(not meaning it)

Go away!

JOE
(joins her at the railing)

I stole forty dollars from your purse.

She sniffles but then turns to him.

NATHALIE

You're that broke?

JOE

It's a temporary thing. It'll be okay tomorrow.

She blows her nose into a napkin and Joe caresses her hair, soothing
her.

NATHALIE

I'm ageing.

JOE

You're a beautiful woman, Nathalie.

NATHALIE
I can't play twenty-three anymore.

JOE
Well, you know, the world moves on.

She presses herself against him.

NATHALIE
You want to stay a while and, you know,
mess around?

JOE
Nathalie, no. Let's not.

She jumps back, angry again.

NATHALIE
Damn it! You see! Even you!

JOE
Nathalie, come on! Every time we make love
there's a fight and then we don't see one
another for—what's it been—three years?

She drops her face into her hands and screams. Then—

NATHALIE
(pathetically)
Why can't I make a man stay?

JOE
Come on, who are you trying to kid! You
don't want a man to stay.

NATHALIE
How do you know!

JOE
How do I know? Because I married you,
remember!

NATHALIE
(realizing)
Oh yeah.

JOE
And you divorced me.

NATHALIE
Yeah, well, I guess when you put it like that...

JOE
Thanks for the forty.

NATHALIE
Is that all you need?

JOE
Yeah.

NATHALIE
The Virgin Mary doesn't have to be matronly,
does she?

JOE
I guess not. I mean, she is a virgin.

NATHALIE
And, of course, she could have had the
Messiah when she was just a very young
girl, right?

JOE
That's how the story goes if I remember
correctly.

All is well. Joe kisses her fondly and leaves.

22. INTERIOR, SUBWAY—DAY

Joe rides the train uptown. He notices that everyone but him is plugged into one sort of digital device or another.

23. EXTERIOR, WASHINGTON HEIGHTS—DAY

Joe comes up out of the subway and crosses west. He comes down the slope of 157th Street to where it joins Riverside Drive. Crossing the street, he enters the leafy courtyard of an apartment building, steps inside to the lobby, and announces himself to the Doorman.

24. INTERIOR, HAL'S APARTMENT—DAY

A middle-aged Hispanic woman, Consuela, is cleaning the bathroom, reaching down with effort and scrubbing the old tub. Spanish language radio plays in the kitchen. She stops when the doorbell rings and goes out to answer it.

> CONSUELA
>
> Mister Joe?

> JOE
>
> *Sí. Hola.* Consuela?

> CONSUELA
>
> *Sí.* Come in.

She allows him in. Entering the studio, he sees the keys to Miho's place waiting for him on the desk. He grabs them and prepares to leave. But he sees Consuela looking with puzzlement at the plug of the vacuum cleaner. She tries to fit the European-sized plug into the American-sized electrical outlet. It doesn't fit.

> JOE
>
> It's a European machine. There must be a
> converter.

She doesn't know what he's talking about but watches as Joe looks around the room.

> JOE
>
> He lived in Europe for a while. All his stuff is
> from over there.
> > *(finds it)*
> Here it is.

Consuela looks on, worried, as he sets the bulky little device on the table and plugs it in.

> JOE
> *(explains)*
> You have to plug that into here. It changes
> the power.

She takes a step back, scared of the heavy little black box. Joe switches it on and it makes an ominous electrical hum. Consuela steps even further back into the hallway, putting the edge of the door between her and the scary machine. Joe considers the vacuum cleaner. He lifts it up onto the table and studies it, impressed, opening and closing its dust compartment and another little hatch where accessories are kept. He nods in approval. Later, in the bedroom, he is vacuuming, analyzing how the machine performs. Consuela is cleaning the windows. Joe switches off the vacuum and hears a news item on the Spanish language radio.

> JOE
> *(of radio)*
> Is this about the girl who jumped off the
> bridge?

> CONSUELA
> Is no girl maybe.

> JOE
> They find the body?

> CONSUELA
> No body.

Finished with the window, she tries to close it. She can't. It won't slide shut easily. And her back hurts. Joe sees this and shakes his head.

> JOE
> Stupid goddamn windows.

He comes over and she lets him wrestle the window closed. With some effort, he does so.

> CONSUELA

Gracias.

> JOE

It would be better if they opened like a door, right? Like this.

He angles his arm and indicates.

> CONSUELA

Sí. Is bad for back, this...
>> *(heads to kitchen, of back)*

Aquí. Malo.

Joe follows her to the kitchen and she pours him a cup of coffee.

> JOE

Thanks.
>> *(of her pain)*

It hurts, huh?

> CONSUELA

Ay, sí.

He places down his cup and steps over just behind her.

> JOE

May I?

> CONSUELA

>> *(tentative)*

Sí.

He lightly touches the center of her lower back. She winces a little and he reacts in kind. Gently, he touches points to the left and right. She nods, feeling he is on the right track.

> CONSUELA

Sí.

                              JOE
          Okay. Let's just—we should do this inside.

Moments later, Consuela is face down on the bed and Joe is expert-
ly massaging her lower back, his hands under her shirt and her jeans
unbuttoned to provide access. For her, it's an orgasmic experience.
But Joe is hard at work.

                              JOE
          Oh, yeah. There it is.

                            CONSUELA
          Ah!!!!!

                              JOE
          That *is* deep.

                            CONSUELA
                           (climaxes)
          Ay, Dios mío!

The Doorman out in the courtyard, hearing the sounds of passion,
glances up at the apartment. But later, Joe and Consuela are at the
kitchen table, calmly finishing their coffee.

                              JOE
          Better, right?

                            CONSUELA
                          (blissed out)
          Sí.

He stands, throws his jacket back on, and prepares to leave. She
watches him like a lover.

                              JOE
          Gotta go. *Gracias.*

25. INTERIOR, SUBWAY—DAY

Joe rides the train back downtown.

                              148

26. INTERIOR, NYC PHONE STORE—DAY

At the counter, Joe buys more minutes for his phone.

> ### SALESGIRL
> How much you want to put on it?

> ### JOE
> Five bucks.

> ### SALESGIRL
> Ten's the minimum.

> ### JOE
> Ten bucks.

27. EXTERIOR, FINANCIAL DISTRICT—DAY

Back out on the sidewalk, Joe makes a call. He waits and someone answers.

> ### JOE
> Jason? Yeah, it's me, Joe. You remember that
> chick, Lori, one of the models in the video we
> made last month? Yeah. She ain't been paid.
> Exactly. What? The check came back in the
> mail? Of course. Okay, tear it up. I'll deal with
> it and invoice you later. Yeah. Okay. See ya.

That done, he hesitates and thinks. Finally, having decided, he dials 911 and waits. Once it's answered—

> ### JOE
> Yeah. Hi. I want to report an incident I think
> might be related to this person who jumped
> off the Brooklyn Bridge earlier today.

28. INTERIOR, MIHO'S APARTMENT—DAY

It's a modern apartment with large windows looking out over the Brooklyn Bridge towards Brooklyn. Joe enters and moves directly to the windows, opens a door, and steps out onto the balcony. He drags a can of beer in a brown paper bag out of his jacket pocket, pops it open, and drinks—relaxing at last. But there's a knock at the door and he comes back in to answer it.

29. INTERIOR, MIHO'S APARTMENT—DAY

Later, Joe is seated at the table while a police officer stands and listens to his description of Amelia. A second officer stands back by the door and looks on.

> JOE
> And, so, she goes on about how a body falling
> from that height would get smashed to pieces
> on the surface of the water. Stuff like that.

> OFFICER
> This was where on the bridge?

> JOE
> *(points)*
> About one third of the way, towards the middle.

> OFFICER
> Brooklyn side?

> JOE
> Right.

> OFFICER
> *(of apartment)*
> You live here?

> JOE
> No. I'm just watching it for my friend, Miho.

> OFFICER
> Last name?

> JOE
> Miho's?

OFFICER

Yeah.

JOE

Hartley.

OFFICER

That's not the name on the buzzer downstairs.

JOE

She sublets it and that's... I don't know...

OFFICER

Not allowed. Where's Miho?

JOE

Shanghai.

OFFICER

She give you the key?

JOE

Her husband did.

OFFICER

And where's he?

JOE

He lives uptown.

OFFICER

Divorced?

JOE

No.

OFFICER

Then why don't she live with him?

JOE

I don't know. She likes it that way, I guess.

OFFICER

What time did you meet this woman on the bridge?

JOE

About eight-fifteen, eight-twenty.

OFFICER

What were you doing on the bridge?

JOE

Walking over here to Manhattan.

OFFICER

Coming here?

JOE

Well yeah sort of.

OFFICER

Sort of?

JOE

I had a meeting. Two meetings.

OFFICER

With who?

JOE

This guy Mike. A broker. But before that I went to my bank.

OFFICER

Real estate broker?

JOE

No, an investment guy. He represents people who invest money in things.

This is getting too complex for the police officer. He glances back at his partner who shrugs. Finally, returning to Joe—

                    OFFICER
        What do you do for a living?

Joe doesn't know how to answer this.

                      JOE
        I'm a drummer.

                    OFFICER
                  (suspicious)
        A drummer?

                      JOE
        I play the drums.

                    OFFICER
                (checks notepad)
        Your business card says you're a producer.

                      JOE
        Yeah, well, I produce video content sometimes
        for an online ad agency too.

                    OFFICER
                (raises an eye brow)
        Oh.

                      JOE
        Maybe a movie in the spring. Too soon to tell.
        I mean...

                    OFFICER
        Is that why you were at the brokerage house?

                      JOE
        What has this got to do with the woman I met
        on the bridge this morning?

                    OFFICER
        Hey! I'm just trying to get an accurate overall
        picture of the situation, okay?

JOE

Sorry.

OFFICER

So, you were at the brokerage house trying
raise money for a movie.

JOE

No. It was—about something else. A business
plan I have. Windows. Importing windows
from Germany.

The officer blinks, overwhelmed. He lifts his cap and massages his
temples. Joe's not sure what's being discussed anymore.

OFFICER

What color hair she have?

JOE

Who?

OFFICER

The woman.

JOE

On the bridge?

OFFICER
(glares at him)
Yeah. The woman on the...

JOE

Brown.

OFFICER

Eyes.

Joe looks from one officer to the other and gives in.

JOE

Dark. Brown, too, I think.

OFFICER

Any other distinguishing features?

JOE

She had a pretty smile.

This unsettles the officer. He hesitates before adding it to his notes. Finally, he does, closes the pad, and gestures to his partner that they're done.

OFFICER

We'll be in touch if we need further
information.

Joe shows them out, relieved. He closes the door and returns to the balcony. He finds his beer and takes a swig. Suddenly, his phone rings and he answers—

JOE

Mike?

MIKE

They like the idea! They want to see a business
plan as soon as possible! Congratulations!

Joe raises his arms triumphantly and stomps his foot.

JOE

I'll get started on the plan. It's all in my head.
I've run the numbers a thousand times.

MIKE

Good. But get in touch with your man Heinrich
in Germany and the architects in Sweden.

JOE

It's night over there now. But I'll email them
right away.

MIKE

Good. Let's talk in the morning.

JOE
Okay. See you later!

He signs off and does a little victory dance.

30. INTERIOR, MIHO'S APARTMENT—NIGHT

Joe works through the night on his business plan, typing on Miho's desktop computer, comparing drafts, scribbling notes on different pages. Well past midnight, he falls asleep in an armchair. He's woken up with a phone call at 3am. He shakes his head clear and answers.

JOE
(into phone)
Bjorn! Yeah. You get my email? Right. We're on. I just need you to specify that the contractor use those windows. Yeah. Call Heinrich in Dusseldorf immediately. He's expecting your call. Okay. Great.

He signs off.

31. INTERIOR, MIHO'S APARTMENT—DAY

The sun comes up and Joe saves his file before hitting print. While the pages of the business plan start sliding out of the copy machine, he steps out on to the balcony to stretch. He realizes he smells. Moments later, he looks through Miho's closet and finds a kimono.

32. INTERIOR, LAUNDRY ROOM—DAY

Down in the building's basement, wearing the kimono as a robe, Joe drags his clothes from a washing machine, dumps them in a dryer, then sits and continues proofreading his business plan.

33. INTERIOR, MIHO'S APARTMENT—DAY

Back upstairs, Joe brushes his teeth, shaves, irons his shirt and polishes his shoes. He ejects a CD from the computer, puts it in a plastic case and neatens the hard copy of the business plan.

Checking the time, he finishes his coffee and leaves.

34. EXTERIOR, FINANCIAL DISTRICT—DAY

Joe walks along with a spring in his step. He dials his cellphone, waits, then—

> ### JOE
> *(into phone)*
> Brother! It's me. Listen, don't do anything
> drastic at work just yet, but I do think I'll be
> needing an experienced business manager.
> Yeah, it looks good. Okay. I'll call you later.
> Thanks.

Joe reaches the pizzeria he plans to meet Lori at. But there is no sign of the girl yet. He checks his watch and steps inside, calling over the counter.

> ### JOE
> Coffee, black. Thanks.

As the guy behind the counter starts to make his coffee, Joe sees Lori wandering around, lost, across the street. He can see she's frustrated and about to walk away. Finally, she does start to walk away. Joe runs out of the pizzeria and into the street, but stops at the sound of tires squealing. Lori stops, too, and looks back. A Taxi Driver who has almost run him down leans out of the taxi and gives Joe the finger. Joe steps back and allows the man to drive on.

35. EXTERIOR, FINANCIAL DISTRICT—DAY

Moments later, Lori stands aside and waits as Joe removes his bank card from his wallet, pauses for breath, and dips it in the ATM.

> ### JOE
> See, everything worked out, right?

> ### LORI
> *(not convinced)*
> We'll see.

He waits and watches the machine expectantly. Finally—

> JOE
>
> Success!

He follows the prompts and goes about making a withdrawal. Lori looks on, amused. But she won't let him see this. Joe eventually counts out the cash and places it in her palm.

> JOE
>
> There you go, young lady: three hundred
> bucks. Do me a favor and don't declare that
> on your taxes. I'm a strictly cash operation.

Satisfied and grateful, she smiles and tucks the cash in her bag.

> LORI
>
> I owe you ten dollars from yesterday, but I
> only have twenties.

> JOE
> *(enjoys negotiating)*
> Actually, you owe me thirteen. But we'll call
> that interest.

> LORI
> *(proudly, pouting)*
> No.

> JOE
>
> Alright, then, buy me a cup of coffee.

> LORI
>
> Okay.

So, a little later, they're seated at the narrow counter looking out onto the street through the plate glass window. Lori savagely devours an egg sandwich as Joe looks on.

> JOE
>
> Easy, good looking, you'll make yourself sick.

She slows down, swallows her last mouthful and washes it back with coffee.

> LORI
> Yesterday morning I stole an apple from a supermarket.

> JOE
> You get away with it?

> LORI
> Yeah. It was easy. My first time in a while.

> JOE
> What, stealing?

> LORI
> No, fruit. Really not interested. But it was the easiest food to steal.

> JOE
> *(impressed)*
> You feeling better now?

> LORI
> Yeah. Fine.

> JOE
> You're not gonna kill yourself or anything, right?

> LORI
> *(embarrassed)*
> Oh, I was just all, you know, emotional. I'm usually really tough.

> JOE
> Oh, really?

> LORI
> Yeah. Everybody says so.

JOE

I'll take your word for it.

LORI

Okay, I'm gonna go get more minutes for my
phone, pay this bitch at NYU so I can get my
shit out of her dorm room, and then go meet
some independent director guy who wants me
to be in his movie.

JOE

Knock 'em dead, sweetheart.

LORI

Oh, I will. Really. I will.

They shake hands and he watches her sashay confidently away. But
then he sees Amelia walk by.

JOE
(jumps up and runs outside)

Hey!

Amelia hasn't heard him and crosses the street at the light.

JOE

Excuse me! Miss!

Now she stops and looks back over her shoulder. Joe, enchanted,
moves off towards her and gets hit by a car. Amelia pales as he rolls
off the hood and collapses in a heap on the pavement. But he lies
there only a moment before he shakes his head clear, rolls up off
the ground and staggers aimlessly away. He collapses into the arms
of two strangers who ease him down onto the sidewalk. A crowd
forms. Amelia kneels down over him. Joe is amazed.

JOE

You're alive.

AMELIA

Easy. You're hurt.

Joe lifts his head, looks down at himself and then up at the crowd surrounding him. Finally, he lays back and sighs.

                    JOE
        I'll live.

The End ~

A/Muse

01. EXTERIOR, BERLIN—DAY

A young women with a suitcase, Christina, stands on the platform at Alexanderplatz Bonhoff, studying her city map. Moments later, she's riding in a train. Finally, she's at a payphone in another part of the city. She dials, waits, then—

> CHRISTINA
> *(in German)*
> Hey! It's me. In Berlin. Thanks.

02. EXTERIOR, BUILDING—DAY

Christina comes up the sidewalk and finds the address she is looking for. She pauses, then enters and passes through to the courtyard and on towards the house at back.

03. INTERIOR, APARTMENT—DAY

Christina is telling her unseen friend why she's in Berlin.

> CHRISTINA
> *(in German)*
> I know he will love me. I believe he will
> like me. I hope he won't think I'm a fool.
> I have watched his films since I was thirteen.
> His actresses; these girls, these women...
> They are like sisters to me. And the men?
> *(thinks about it)*
> They have taught me to love what is not easy
> or convenient.
> *(hand on heart, moved)*
> These are my people.
> *(lifts a bowl of strawberries)*
> If he can see me, or just hear me... I will be
> his new actress. The new girl. I'm perfectly
> confident.
> *(devouring strawberries)*
> Of course, he will have to make films in
> German. But I can convince him. I think he
> wants this. He's ready. Why else is he, an

American, living in Berlin? The shopkeeper
downstairs says he's often not home.
                  (grins mischievously)
There's a girl, apparently, in Friedrichshain
or Kreuzberg.
                  (one last strawberry, then)
They say he is directing a play in the East.
How do I get there?

04. EXTERIOR, BERLIN—DAY

Christina makes her way to the East. She stops and has her picture
taken in an old automatic coin-operated photobooth.

05. EXTERIOR, THEATER—DAY

She talks with an angry technician outside the theater. He throws
up his hands and walks off. Disappointed, she finds a payphone
and talks to her friend, in German.

                  CHRISTINA
He fought with the technicians and left. They
don't know when he'll be back. He does this
all the time, I guess. Someone said he always
eats at the same restaurant near Schonehauser-
allee.

06. EXTERIOR, RESTAURANT—DAY

Christina waits expectantly at a table outside a small cafe, watching different men coming and going. But she does not see the one
she is searching for.

07. INTERIOR, TRAIN—DAY

Despondent, Christina rides the S-Bahn back to the apartment.

                  CHRISTINA
              (voice over, in German)
They say he returned to America. There's a
post office box in New York.

08. INTERIOR, APARTMENT—DAY

Christina sets herself up at a desk and prepares to write a letter on her laptop. But her English is clumsy.

> CHRISTINA
> Dear Sir. Dear Mister. I am a girl. I am the
> girl. I am a girl... No. I am an actress.
>> *(starts over)*
> Dear Sir. I am an actress from the small
> German town of Mittlekreuz. Me and my
> sisters have loved your films since we were
> young. Since we were children. Sadly, we
> were disliked for this, but came to appreciate
> the joys of the... migrant... No, the outsider.
>> *(paces back and forth)*
> I am intellectual. I am intellectual, talented,
> hardworking and.... pretty.
>> *(corrects this)*
> Some say I am pretty. I will include my
> picture.
>> *(chooses the best of her*
>> *photobooth pictures)*
> I want to be the leading lady in your first
> great German film.
>> *(types all this, then)*
> Postscript. PS. You can reply to me at the
> address provided. With great friendship and...
>> *(dissatisfied, she gets up*
>> *and paces again, returning*
>> *to the laptop with emotion)*
> Write to me also to relieve your mind of the
> heavy thoughts and lonesome memories I
> know great geniuses are never without.
>> *(reads this, then adds)*
> Especially in exile.

09. EXTERIOR, BUILDING—DAY

Some weeks have passed. Christina checks the mailbox and finds a reply to her letter.

10. EXTERIOR, BERLIN—DAY

She finds a secluded park bench, sits, and pauses before opening the letter. Finally, she reads.

> CHRISTINA
> *(voice over, in English)*
> Dear Miss. Thank you for your letter and
> picture. I am afraid my great German film will
> not happen. My years in Berlin, however, were
> not the exile you imagine them to be. Maybe
> you should make that great German film you
> imagine I would have made. Me, I'm in the
> window business these days. I have been so
> impressed with these excellently designed
> and manufactured windows here in Europe.
> I have started to import them to the United
> States and have hopes of providing them to a
> few major building contractors. Wish me luck.
> Our time is our own and the beauty we create
> from it is up to us. *Auf Weidersehen.*

Finishing this letter, standing by a pond, Christina is almost too weak to stand.

11. INTERIOR, APARTMENT—DAY

Later, she has thrown herself down on the couch and lies there, disconsolate, until she finds the energy to stand up and remove her coat. Dropping her coat to the floor, she notices the windows. She approaches and—with extreme care and attention—opens and closes one. She, too, is impressed.

12. EXTERIOR, BERLIN—DAY

Christina is at another payphone outside Zoo Station, talking to her unseen friend, in German.

> CHRISTINA
> I'm leaving. No, Paris. Someone will discover
> their genius in my face, my hands, the sound

of my voice! I have a duty to make this happen...
What?
(hears train)
Oh, my train is coming. Bye!

She hangs up and runs into the station.

The End ~

Apologies

01. INTERIOR, APARTMENT—DAY

Nikolai is a thirty-five-year-old American man on the balcony of his apartment overlooking Berlin. He gestures grandly and quotes from the classics into his cellphone with someone half a world away.

> NIKOLAI
>
> "I know well how men in exile feed
> on dreams of hope."
> *(listens, then)*
> No. No, that's Aeschylus. So, listen,
> I can be there in the morning. Yeah,
> there's a connection I can make in
> London tonight. I've already called
> a taxi. In the meantime, I'll work on
> the second act. Look, don't worry, my
> friend! So, the show's a disaster. We
> can fix it. We've been in worse scrapes
> before, right? Yeah, I'll write some
> new dialogue, invent some action,
> special effects. Nudity? Yeah, I'm not
> above that sort of thing. Listen, this
> will be the best musical version of *The
> Odyssey* ever—at least in English.
> Yeah, okay. Hang in there. I'll see you
> tomorrow. Okay. Bye.

02. INTERIOR, APARTMENT—DAY

While he waits for the taxi, Nikolai acts out a possible scene for his revision, jotting down notes as he goes.

> NIKOLAI
>
> Enter the king! The messenger is waiting
> impatiently. The king sits.
> *(he sits)*
> He hangs his head.
> *(he hangs his head)*
> He studies his hands. The messenger
> approaches.

Nikolai jumps up and rushes to the far side of the table to play the part of the Messenger, leaning over towards where the king is supposedly sitting.

NIKOLAI
(as Messenger)
When will this end? Relent! Your father, the
king...
(looks aside)
Wait a minute. *He's* the king.

He returns to his seat and starts all over again.

NIKOLAI
Enter the king! The messenger is waiting
impatiently. The king sits. He hangs his
head. He studies his hands. The Messenger
approaches.
(runs around the table)
When will this end? Relent! Your father calls
you back himself! Your wife, the Queen, that
most whatever of beautiful females, etcetera,
etcetera, surrounded by gutless riffraff
advocating divorce proceedings and a separate
apartment downtown!

He stops. He has ideas. He writes them down.

NIKOLAI
Period. Contemporary and also... *not*. Who
are the gutless riffraff? Penelope should be a
lawyer or some sort of high-blown sales rep.

He sets down his pen and looks across the room to where another
him is preparing to leave.

NIKOLAI
(challenges him)
What has all this been for? A new realm to
conquer? For what? You are as invisible here
as you were at home amongst your own people.

The Other Nikolai nods, agreeing.

> OTHER
> I was not what I promised.

> NIKOLAI
> You changed.

> OTHER
> *(insists)*
> No! It was the *world* that changed.

> NIKOLAI
> The world is always changing. But it
> stays the same.

> OTHER
> It expects nothing less from its
> commodities.

> NIKOLAI
> Stop complaining.

03. INTERIOR, APARTMENT—DAY

Later, Nikolai is in the front hall. He puts on his coat, checks his wallet, cellphone, and luggage. He sighs and studies an illuminated globe that acts as a lamp.

> NIKOLAI
> Yes, of course, the people deserve a
> sustainable entertainment industry. An
> economy sufficient unto itself.
> *(sits and laces his shoe)*
> Not a culture that requires constant
> encouragement.
> *(leans back and sighs)*
> What was I thinking?

He looks aside, frowns, and starts composing dialogue out loud again, unable to stop working—

NIKOLAI
Go! Go as the lightning before thunder...
(dissatisfied, stops, then)
Stillness! Stillness before the...
(gives up again)
No. I've used that already.
(answers ringing cellphone)
Yeah, hello? Okay, I'll be right down.

He turns off the lights, grabs his luggage and prepares to leave. Pulling open the door, he pauses and glances back at a small suitcase left standing in the hallway. He leaves it there and exits.

04. INTERIOR, APARTMENT—DAY

Later, a timid young woman, Ireen, lets herself into Nikolai's apartment with a key of her own. She has not been here before. She removes her coat and hangs it up, then looks curiously at the little suitcase left there in the hallway. She notices a note on the hallway table beside the globe lamp.

IREEN
(reads)
"Thanks for looking after the place. Good luck
with your audition. My ex-girlfriend will
come by to return her keys and take away the
suitcase in the hall."

Ireen ventures further into the apartment and looks around. She's intrigued by Nikolai's notebook lying, forgotten, on the table. Lifting it, she pages through and stops at a certain passage.

IREEN
(reads)
"I am pushed along by circumstances I somehow helped create, but which I am never in
control of."

Feeling she's intruded, she closes the book and puts it back down. She wanders around the place, looking into the rooms, tinkering with Nikolai's musical instruments.

05. INTERIOR, APARTMENT—DAY

Finally, Ireen settles down at the kitchen table, has some tea, and reads aloud from a collection of audition pieces for actresses, *Monologen fur Frauen.*

> IREEN
> *(in German)*
> "It was so beautiful. Do you ever think about
> it? Yes, you have hurt me, alas. But what does
> not end in pain? Good days, I have seen few.
> But the ones I have seen are like a dream. The
> flowers in the window, my flowers! The fragile
> little spinet. The box I kept your letters in and
> whatever little gifts you gave me. All of it.
> Don't laugh. All of it became beautiful."

She closes the book, bored, and looks at the suitcase in the hall. She stands and approaches it, curious. Finally, she kneels down, lays it on its side and opens it. She finds an elaborate period costume gown and some sheer stockings. She lifts them out and studies them.

06. INTERIOR, APARTMENT—DAY

Later, she is wearing the dress and lying on the couch, reciting the monologue from memory but as if she were in an action film, firing an imaginary pistol at different corners of the room and dodging bullets.

> IREEN
> *(in German)*
> "Don't laugh at me! All of it became beautiful
> and spoke in the language of love! In the
> sultry evening rain!"

07. INTERIOR, APARTMENT—DAY

Later still, in Nikolai's studio, Ireen is swaying dreamily before an old-fashioned microphone, whispering the monologue intensely, intimately, desperately—

IREEN
(in German)
"When your last and worst letter came,
I wanted to die. I don't say this to hurt you.
I wanted to write you a letter without
complaining. Not harsh, without sadness, but
only so you should be homesick for me and
our love, and cry because it is too late. But I
didn't write you anyway. No. Why should I?
How do I know how much of your heart you
put into what made me so happy? I walked
around in a daydream. Nothing will make the
unfaithful faithful, and tears will not resurrect
anything. You don't even die of this! After this
long, boring suffering I could have allowed
myself to lay down and die. But I asked to be
with you in *your* time of dying."

08. INTERIOR, APARTMENT—DAY

Sometime later, Ireen is sprawled on the floor alongside a lamp,
speaking to it tenderly, as if to someone wounded.

IREEN
(in German)
"Good days, I have seen a few. But the ones I
have seen are like a dream. The flowers in
the window. My flowers. The fragile little
spinet. The box I kept your letters in..."

But she stops abruptly, hearing the rattling of keys and the locks
turning on the front door. Panicked, and with no time to remove
the dress, she runs into the kitchen and locks herself in. A sophisticated and beautiful women, Bettina, enters the apartment. She
looks around for Nikolai, doesn't see him, and tries the kitchen
door. Discovering it's locked and hearing some movement within,
she hangs her set of keys on the coat rack and sighs.

BETTINA
(tenderly)
It's me. Come out.

Inside, Ireen is huddled under the kitchen table, hiding behind her knees. Getting no response, Bettina decides it doesn't matter and wanders around the apartment while she addresses Nikolai out loud.

BETTINA
(wistful)

No, it's better this way. Stay there. I don't
want you to see me disappointed.
(crosses to his library)
You have only flirted with me. Led me on.
Flattered me with your concern for my
opinion. But when my opinion was no longer
useful, you carried on as you wanted. A voice
crying out in the wilderness.
(absently studies a book)
Your vanity prevents you from seeing how
passive enthusiasts with a sense of entitlement,
require trusted and well-paid intermediaries.
(returns to kitchen door)
You spurn me now for the same reasons you
loved me.
*(presses herself against the door,
quietly passionate)*
Still, I do not regret having given you the
best reviews you deserved at the time.
(steps back, controls herself)
You were what you promised, but nothing
more.
(of suitcase in hallway)
I'm leaving the dress and the fancy lingerie.
I only did that for you.
(at entrance, leaving)
Auf Weidersehen. Adieu. Goodbye.

And she lets herself out.

Ireen is desperately relieved and climbs out from under the kitchen table. She runs through the apartment and out onto the balcony to see Bettina walk away in the street below. Satisfied, she relaxes and confidently displays herself in the elegant dress.

IREEN
(defiantly, in German)
Nothing will make the unfaithful faithful!
And tears will not resurrect anything!

The End ~

Accomplice

01. INTERIOR, APARTMENT—DAY

It is a dark, grey winter morning in Berlin. A demure young woman, Jordana, enters the apartment and turns on the light in the
library. She sorts the mail and finds a small package with two
videotapes. She steps out onto the balcony to have a smoke and
we hear a voice message she's received from her Boss.

BOSS

Mon amie.
The night becomes day, I guess.
Even in Berlin.
(down to business)
I stole some tapes from the museum
in Minneapolis in nineteen ninety-two.
They'll reach you in Berlin on Tuesday.
Copy them to the hard drive, make
duplicates, and erase the originals.
There have been complications.
I expect you to confront them with your
customary ruthlessness.

02. INTERIOR, APARTMENT—DAY

A few days later, while Jordana is in fact copying the tapes and
destroying the originals, she listens obediently to some German
official explaining import tax violations.

OFFICIAL

(in German)
The paperwork was not completed
correctly for the importation of filmed
entertainment as stipulated in line six
of Form 47-A and so the item must be
sent back and shipped to Germany
again in a manner consistent with the
regulations. Three copies of the
documents must be submitted...

Jordana just blinks innocently and lets the man explain the rules in
impossible detail. We also hear more of her Boss' message—

BOSS
Apart from crime, I think of you often.
The law, of course, is everywhere and my
transgressions well known.

The post office official finally leaves and she checks the copy she
has made of the contraband video. It is an interview with the
Swiss-French filmmaker, Jean-Luc Godard. He sits and listens to
a question posed by the film critic, David Bordwell.

BORDWELL
To what extent do you see your work as
exploring some of the things that audiences
already expect to find in films? That is, when
someone comes to a movie, they expect a
love story, they expect conflicts—problems
of the characters. To what extent do you
want to use what people are expecting to see
in your own work?

Godard considers the question.

03. INTERIOR, APARTMENT—DAY

The following afternoon, Jordana listens to the audio of Godard's
reply through headphones as she neatens up the apartment.

GODARD
(voice over)
After all, I say I am innocently representing
a certain belief in motion pictures. We will
always be able to do a small movie with
friends and to show to someone. Okay, you
won't get the Oscar for this! But, after all,
why are you writing, and *why* are you...
(let's it go, moves on)
So it will be possible. I have always said that
to make movies, to make images and sound,
is possible, one way or another.

Jordana pauses and considers this. Then she notices the daylight lessening and checks the time on her wristwatch.

04. EXTERIOR, APARTMENT—DAY

Later, as the evening descends, Jordana is out on the balcony with her mobile phone, waiting to make a call, watching a restaurant's unlighted neon sign across the street which reads, *Bar Americain*. Meanwhile, we hear the last of her Boss' message.

> BOSS
> *(tender)*
> Call me when the coast is clear.
> At the moment of our sign.

The sign is turned on. It lights up and so Jordana makes her call. It's answered.

> JORDANA
> *(happy, into phone)*

Hey!

> BOSS
> *(elegiac, off)*
> Fugitive, uprooted, adrift,
> I wait.
> Still threatened by this intimacy,
> These small favors,
> This weight we choose to bear.

The End ~

CPSIA information can be obtained
at www.ICGtesting.com
Printed in the USA
FSHW022342150421